FIVE COLLEGE COOPERATION

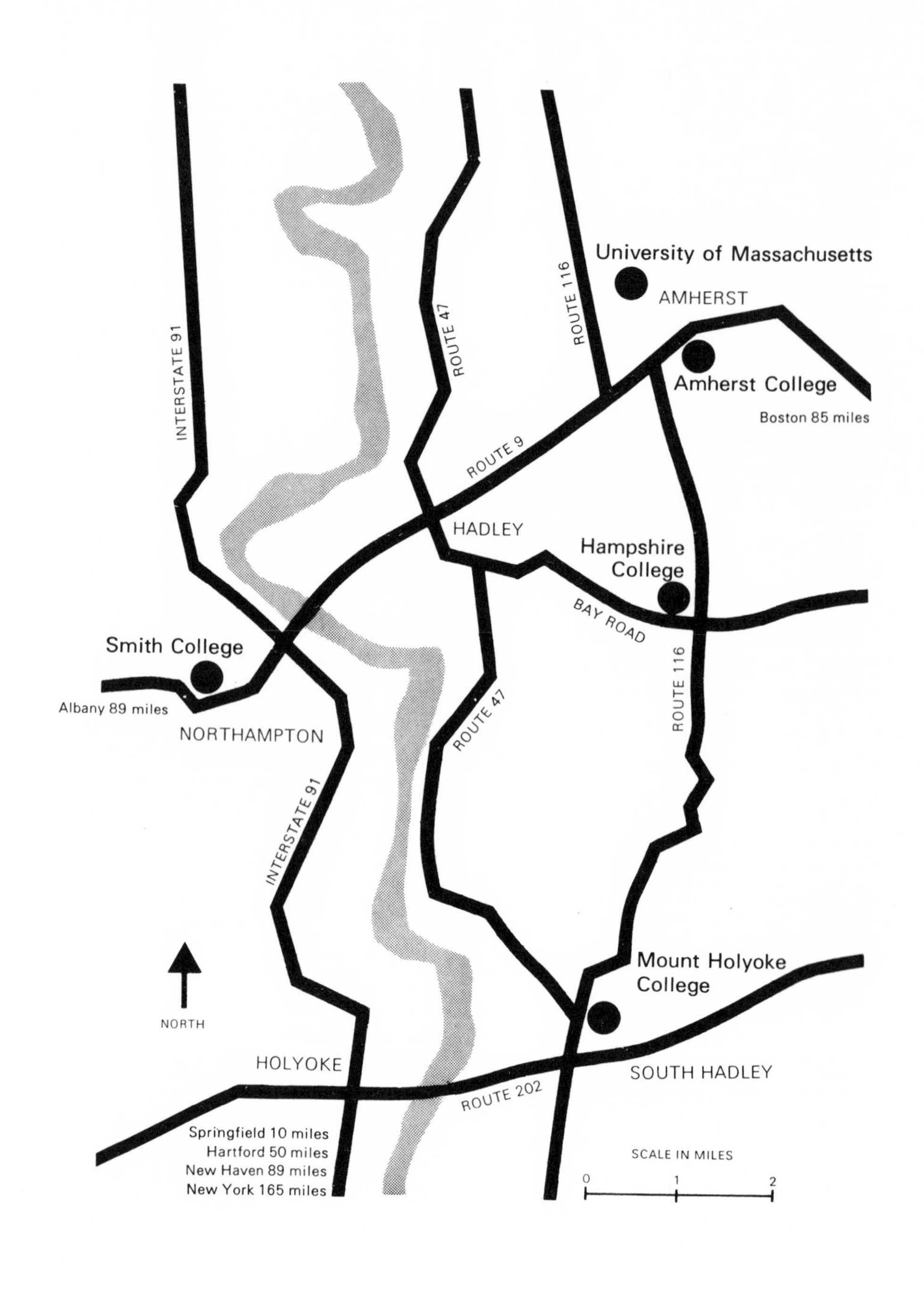
University of Massachusetts
AMHERST
Amherst College
Boston 85 miles
ROUTE 116
ROUTE 47
INTERSTATE 91
ROUTE 9
HADLEY
Hampshire College
BAY ROAD
ROUTE 116
Smith College
Albany 89 miles
NORTHAMPTON
ROUTE 47
INTERSTATE 91
NORTH
Mount Holyoke College
HOLYOKE
SOUTH HADLEY
ROUTE 202
Springfield 10 miles
Hartford 50 miles
New Haven 89 miles
New York 165 miles
SCALE IN MILES
0
1
2

Five College Cooperation

Directions for the Future

Report of the Five College Long Range Planning Committee 1969

AMHERST COLLEGE

HAMPSHIRE COLLEGE

MOUNT HOLYOKE COLLEGE

SMITH COLLEGE

UNIVERSITY OF MASSACHUSETTS

Additional copies of this volume
may be ordered from
The University of Massachusetts Press
Amherst, Massachusetts 01002
at $5.00 each.

Library of Congress Catalog Card Number 72–100059
Set in Baskerville types by Westcott & Thomson, Inc.
and printed in the United States of America by
Halliday Lithograph Corporation

Letter of Transmittal

October, 1969

John W. Lederle, President, University of Massachusetts
Thomas C. Mendenhall, President, Smith College
Franklin Patterson, President, Hampshire College
Calvin H. Plimpton, President, Amherst College
David B. Truman, President, Mount Holyoke College

Gentlemen:

The Five College Long Range Planning Committee (LRPC) was appointed by the Presidents of the five colleges in the spring of 1968 to make an extensive review of present cooperative arrangements among the five institutions, assess their strengths and weaknesses, propose long-range goals for cooperation, and establish priorities among actions required to reach those goals. Its membership included the Five College Coordinator, who served as Chairman, and three people from each institution: a faculty member who had held positions of trust within his own faculty, a high-ranking academic administrator, and the chief business officer.

The Committee met in July, 1968, for two four-day weekends, during the academic year 1968–69 on the second and fourth Friday evening of each month, and for several days during the early summer of 1969. The three subgroups into which it divided itself often met at additional times with various committees, subcommittees, and interested individual faculty members, administrators, and students. A Planning Liaison Group was set up in November, consisting of the Chairman of the LRPC, the Chairmen of its three subgroups, and four students from the Five College Student

Coordinating Board (FCSCB). This group met every two or three weeks to maintain liaison between the LRPC and the FCSCB.

Many people have assisted in the preparation of this report. Some of them are named in the Acknowledgements. To them and the many more not listed, the Committee extends its thanks. The Committee owes a particular debt of gratitude to its Staff Assistant, Miss Barbara Turlington, who both organized its work and contributed greatly to the report.

The Committee would also like to express its appreciation to the U. S. Steel Foundation for a grant in 1968 which helped underwrite the costs of the Committee, and to the Trustees of the Richard K. Mellon Trusts for a grant which will be used primarily to assist in carrying out those recommendations in this report having to do with academic programs.

Each one of the sixteen members of the LRPC, and its Staff Assistant as well, contributed draft papers for this report. All drafts were discussed and revised by the Committee, and all members have read and accepted the entire report. This, then, is in every sense a product of the Committee as a whole.

Although the report deals only with the five colleges, the Committee considered reports from other academic consortia as well. It may be that the principles developed here will be useful for other institutions of higher education which are engaged in cooperative undertakings.

The LRPC urges all members of the five-college community to discuss this report and its various recommendations in the hope that they may reach agreement not only on the general principles espoused, but also on the particular steps proposed. This process should begin this fall, so that decisions on as many recommendations as possible may be reached by the end of this academic year. Many matters will require further study, and the document itself should be reviewed regularly if it is to have continued meaning. Accordingly, the LRPC urges that long-range planning of the cooperative enterprise be continued throughout the five-college community in the future.

The Committee hopes that this report may assist all of our institutions better to serve their students and faculties and the wider communities of which they are part.

Sincerely yours,

Robert C. Birney, Hampshire College
North Burn, Five College Coordinator
David M. Clay, University of Massachusetts
Robert L. Ellis, Smith College
Prosser Gifford, Amherst College
Theodore P. Greene, Amherst College
William C. Havard, Jr., University of Massachusetts
Charles Henderson, Jr., Smith College
Kurt M. Hertzfeld, Amherst College
Charles R. Longsworth, Hampshire College
Richard C. Lyon, Hampshire College
George F. Mair, Smith College
Leo F. Redfern, University of Massachusetts
Lawrence E. Remillard, Mount Holyoke College
John L. Teall, Mount Holyoke College
Mary E. Tuttle, Mount Holyoke College

Table of Contents

Introduction

A. History of Cooperation

Cooperation among the institutions of higher education in the central Connecticut Valley began with the founding of the colleges. Mount Holyoke College, Smith College, and the original Massachusetts Agricultural College in Amherst were all assisted in their early days by faculty members and administrators from Amherst College. This report concerns cooperation among these four long-established institutions and one new one, Hampshire College, which will open in 1970.

In 1914 a Committee on University Extension of the Connecticut Valley Colleges was established, composed of representatives from Amherst, Mount Holyoke, Smith, Springfield College (then the International Y.M.C.A. College), and the University (then the Massachusetts Agricultural College). This committee cooperated in initiating and staffing extension courses throughout western Massachusetts and elsewhere, organized leadership training courses for workers in Holyoke, Chicopee, and Springfield, and helped to organize Holyoke Junior College. It also provided consultants to the Pittsfield Engineering Program (1949–58) and to the Westover Air Force Base Program of college courses. In 1922–23 it sponsored the first courses of instruction given by radio in this country and later took an active part in the organization and incorporation of the Western Massachusetts Educational Television Council. The committee continued its work until 1958.

The three colleges and the University also had informal

programs of faculty and student exchange from at least the 1930's on. Students occasionally took at another institution advanced courses not available to them on their home campus. There was considerable overtime borrowing of faculty, and there were occasional direct faculty exchanges.

There had been cooperation among the libraries for a long period, and the first formal jointly supported facility was the Hampshire Inter-Library Center, established in 1951 as a four-college depository of expensive and infrequently used books and periodicals.

In 1956 a committee of faculty members from the four institutions, supported by a grant from the Fund for the Advancement of Education, produced a study of other possible cooperative arrangements, ranging from programs of cooperation and joint appointments in undergraduate instruction in particular departments through the establishment of an educational FM radio station, coordination of lectures and concerts, joint programs in remedial reading and speech therapy, encouragement of joint graduate programs and cooperative area programs, to the appointment of a Coordinator to administer the various cooperative arrangements. The first Coordinator was appointed in 1957. The present Coordinator, appointed in the fall of 1967, is the fourth.

Although some of the proposals of the 1956 *Report of the Committee on Cooperation* were never implemented, much progress was made in cooperative programs. Astronomy was developed as a joint department and now offers one of the best programs in the country. Several joint appointments of faculty have been made, as in History of Science and, for limited periods, in some non-Western area studies. There is a cooperative Ph.D. program which has been especially successful in the sciences, with students in residence at one institution able to make use of the resources and faculty of another. Two Ford Foundation grants totaling $506,000 made possible the expansion of Asian and African Studies at all four institutions on a cooperative basis, supporting library acquisitions, visiting scholars and lecturers, and faculty seminars and research projects.

An educational FM radio station (WFCR) was established and receives support from all of the institutions, as does the *Massachusetts Review*. A Four College Calendar of Events was initiated to make available information on lectures, concerts, and other activities on all campuses. Student course exchange has increased each year, growing from 105 in 1957 to over 1,000 in 1968–69. A number of departments work closely together to share information on courses and faculty. Several interinstitutional faculty seminars have attracted faculty members from all the institutions.

The 1956 *Report of the Committee on Cooperation* aroused nationwide interest among institutions of higher education. The cooperative effort was one of the earliest in the country and the first to include both private colleges and a state university. Since then, more than fifty other consortia with professional staffs have been formed among institutions of higher education. The Coordinator's Office receives numerous requests for information and advice from institutions planning new cooperative arrangements.

In 1958 another four-college committee recommended the establishment of a fifth college in the Valley, to be located centrally to the other four and designed to take advantage of their presence while trying new ways of educating students which might prove of value to the others. The resulting *New College Plan* was widely circulated. In 1965 an Amherst alumnus offered six million dollars with which to begin what came to be called Hampshire College, which will open in the fall of 1970. A four-college committee to advise the President of Hampshire College was appointed in 1966.

In the spring of 1968 the five Presidents established the Five College Long Range Planning Committee, which includes representatives of the faculties and administrations of all five institutions. The Committee was directed to review the strengths and weaknesses of present cooperative programs and, in consultation with faculty, student, and administrative groups, to make recommendations for the future of cooperation among the institutions. This report is the result of the work of that Committee during the past year.

B. Reasons for Cooperation

THE PURPOSE of all academic consortia is to strengthen educational offerings by more effectively allocating and conserving limited resources of money, staff, and facilities. Most groups have found that they can not only improve and strengthen their present programs but also add educational and administrative programs that no single institution might have been able to introduce on its own.

The Long Range Planning Committee has drawn up its recommendations in the light of certain observations about what has been happening and will be happening in the field of higher education generally and in the Valley in particular. We believe that these developments increase both the need and the opportunities for cooperation.

All institutions of higher education are facing rapidly increasing costs in salaries, buildings, books, and other instructional materials. They cannot assume, as industries do, that advancing technology and increased investment will enable them to produce more of their "product" at lower proportional cost. Further, they are faced with an accelerating growth in knowledge and a steady increase in the number of academic fields that their faculty and students want to explore. New programs and new kinds of research techniques must be added if these institutions are to remain viable. But new programs are expensive. New tools, such as computers and video tape, can increase what can be done, but they also are expensive. These new programs and facilities are especially appropriate for cooperative development, partly because of their expense, but also because they do not appear to threaten the self-interest of established departments at the member institutions. This is also true of the development of new research and study facilities away from the campus, such as overseas institutes, urban centers, and the like, for which there is increasing demand by both students and faculty.

There are other areas in which cooperation might help the institutions improve existing programs but in which implementation is difficult because it does appear to threaten the autonomy of the institution or of individuals or groups within it. For instance, some smaller departments might develop better programs if they cooperated in joint hiring of some faculty members with advanced specialties, or divided some of their more advanced courses among the various institutions to provide their students with a wider variety of experience with both professors and fellow students, or to increase very small classes of three or four students to a critical size of eight or ten, thus permitting broader coverage and better discussion. Other departments, such as some in the sciences, might be better able to provide some of the expensive equipment which their advanced students need for research if they were to agree to share it.

Such cooperative efforts are difficult where distances between the institutions make travel time a factor. They are impossible unless there is communication and consultation among people who know each other and have respect for each other's competence. This kind of communication and respect is built up slowly over a period of time; it depends not only on individual contacts but on the whole climate surrounding the cooperative enterprise. For this reason, most successful cooperative endeavors have begun with fairly limited and specific projects rather than with general plans.

No member of the Long Range Planning Committee wishes to see the four colleges and the University move toward complete merger. Despite their many similarities, each of the five institutions has a concept of its individual role in education. Each has its own identity, each its own style. Some of these distinctive characteristics are manifest in such differences as size, range of academic offerings, nature of the student body, architectural style, financial resources, administrative mechanics, course schedules, and calendars. Other distinctions are less perceptible and exceedingly difficult to state exactly but are nonetheless real. They are differences in approach, in attitude, in what might be described as atmosphere. Some of these intangible qualities reflect long traditions, strong personalities, or mere habit; others are the result of deliberate planning. This complex of attributes and attitudes is therefore not easily changed—nor should it be—but it is not impervious to change, as the last twenty years in the University's rise to major university status will testify.

In this report the LRPC has regarded this diversity, this sense of difference, as one of the Valley's strongest educational assets, and one to be preserved and built upon as we seek to make the best use of our resources. To be sure, in some of the recommendations dealing with mechanical and procedural matters, the report calls for a certain degree of standardized and orderly administrative action. But it is the Committee's belief that these orderly procedures are the best means to preserve and develop even further, in practical ways, the special excellences of the several institutions.

Some special reasons exist for cooperation among the Valley colleges, and there are special benefits to be gained. One of the new problems that we all face is that many of the more capable and interesting students whom we would like to recruit are more attracted to urban environments. Despite our relatively rural setting, we can provide, with cooperative efforts, a very broad range of cultural events and lectures. In addition, we can offer a wide range of courses concerned with urban problems and a cooperatively supported field office in a nearby urban center.

One of the most insistent student demands at the present time is for coeducation. Although no one can predict whether the three single-sex institutions in the Valley will be fully coeducational in the future, we do accept the assumption that all three will respond in some way to this pressure, perhaps in a variety of ways. Committees at all three colleges are studying the question, with varying degrees of urgency.

If the single-sex colleges choose not to become coeducational, five-college cooperation may enable them to develop distinctive patterns, so that they can both retain the advantages of their present system and achieve some of the advantages of coeducation. In any case, student and faculty exchange may allow them to delay a decision to become coeducational until they can evaluate the experiences of other institutions which are now doing so and the effects of such changes on their own applications and enrollments. On the other hand, if one or more of these colleges do make the decision to become coeducational, five-college cooperation should help them in their effort to attract and hold the kind of students they want.

New outside pressures will also be put on higher education. There are pressures upon colleges and universities to increase the diversity of the population from which they draw their students. The Valley institutions are committed to increased recruitment from disadvantaged groups and must deal with the financial and other problems which such recruitment implies. In addition, society is now demanding more in the way of direct services from colleges and universities than it has since the early days of agricultural extension services. Educational institutions are asked to help with urban problems and city planning, with health services and problems of pollution. Most of them are already responding to these demands, but it can be expected that the demands will continue to grow. Cooperation offers a way of dealing with them more effectively and more responsibly in ways appropriate for the institutions.

The LRPC anticipates that the role of the University in cooperative programs will become increasingly problematic and complex as the University approaches its projected enrollment of thirty thousand students and as it further develops both undergraduate and graduate course offerings. On the other hand, the University has special reasons for cooperation with the colleges. Its President has pointed out that it is a great advantage for students at the University, who are predominantly from Massachusetts, to have contact with the more diverse student bodies of the colleges. From the academic point of view, the colleges will always have highly qualified scholars in particular specialties which the University may be unable to offer. These scholars could be used by the University's graduate schools as well as by qualified undergraduate students. The colleges can also assist the University in its public service role, in cooperative efforts on lecture series, adult education workshops, and the improvement of secondary school and community college education.

The maintenance of independence and self-direction for educational institutions at a time of rapid change and deep division over social values in the society at large requires patient, reiterated explanation of the purposes of higher education. The need to present to legislatures and alumni the renewed desirability of institutional independence from immediate demands—those of radical students and those of outraged outsiders—unites public and private institutions of higher learning in new ways. The careful reassertion of the integrity and responsibility of colleges and universities and of their dedication to critical and original inquiry can gain greatly from cooperation between public and private institutions.

The colleges have a number of important reasons for cooperating with the University. First, the University, given its size and funds, can offer a much wider variety of courses than the colleges. Second, many observers see an increasing trend on the part of faculty members to seek the opportunity to work with graduate students and to have graduate student assistants in laboratories and as readers. Although the Academic Deans at some of the colleges expect to have no difficulty in attracting excellent faculty members solely for undergraduate teaching, for those faculty members whose academic specialties and inclinations do require contact with graduate students, graduate faculties, and highly specialized research materials, opportunities to participate in the University's graduate programs offer real advantages.

In a few years, Hampshire College will have a full student body. Hampshire has been planned from the beginning to demonstrate how a new undergraduate college may benefit from cooperation with established neighboring institutions. Thus it is assumed that most Hampshire students will take some courses at the other colleges and the University. Hampshire, in turn, will contribute to the cooperative enterprise by offering special facilities and courses to students from the other campuses.

The new college may also present some problems. The other institutions must take into account the potential impact of a new, innovative institution in their midst, with different academic programs and different academic organization. Hampshire College will have to consider in its planning the possibility that too great differences in program and organization may create new problems for cooperation.

Finally, in our survey of reasons for cooperation, we note that increasing financial pressures on institutions of higher education are generally recognized as a major problem. New sources of funds, including federal and state governments, will have to be found, and new ways of saving money must be sought. Although the primary purpose of cooperation is not to save money, but to improve the use of educational resources, there are aspects of cooperation which will be helpful in meeting the financial problems of all the institutions.

We believe that the combination of all of these factors will make five-college cooperation even more important in the future than it has been in the past. It may also make cooperation more difficult. As financial, social, and academic pressures push the colleges and the University into attempts to develop more complementary programs, not only will the five-college community need to develop some new decision-making machinery; it will need to develop some new attitudes. Some of this is already occurring, as discussed below. The Committee hopes that some of its recommendations may help to make this process both more rational and more adequate to the increasing demands upon us all.

C. Limitations & Obstacles

One of the problems mentioned at many conferences and in studies of institutional cooperation is that the official reports of academic consortia seldom discuss the limitations of cooperation, focusing instead on the possibilities. This may be because some of the reports reserve the knottier problems for private memoranda to the directors or Presidents of the institutions. The LRPC considered this possibility, but decided that some of the problems could best be solved if they were faced squarely by the whole community. We will mention in the body of the report a number of problems. Here we wish to discuss specifically some of the more sensitive ones.

There are very real problems and legitimate restraints in any attempt by diverse institutions to develop cooperative plans and programs. These become especially difficult where the cooperative endeavor includes both relatively small private colleges and a rapidly expanding public university. The aims and needs of the institutions, although frequently complementary, will in some cases conflict.

It is probably unrealistic, for example, to expect a growing university to make binding agreements not to expand into fields it does not presently cover, and to continue to depend on coverage of these fields by the colleges. Temporary arrangements may be made in such fields, and consultation can be expected and indeed enforced, but the self-limitation process could become so restrictive that the institution rebels.

Another problem is the possibility of differences in standards among institutions. This affects relations even among departments at the same institution, of course, and among the colleges, but it is particularly sensitive in relation to the University. The University of necessity accepts a larger proportion of students with less adequate preparation and lower test scores than do the colleges. It has so far attracted somewhat fewer students with very high test scores—over 700 on the College Board Scholastic Aptitude Test (SAT), for instance. Faculty members at the colleges express some concern that courses at the University may not meet the same standards as those at the colleges and that exchange students from the University may not be so well prepared as their own students.

The former fear tends to diminish in direct relation to the degree to which college faculty members are in contact with their colleagues at the University. Growing confidence in University courses and faculty has been shown in recent years by the increasing number of students from the colleges enrolled in exchange courses at the University and by the number of faculty borrowed from the University to teach courses at the colleges. If there is any difference in standards of course work, it is probably found mainly among introductory courses.

Examination of SAT scores of entering freshmen at the University and at the colleges shows that the University has a large number of students with middle-to-high-range scores. There is, in fact, a larger number of freshmen at the University with SAT scores over 600 than at any one of the colleges. The grade records of exchange students show that students from the University have done as well as or better than students from the home college and that private college students did no better at the University than at home. Since even under a liberalized policy of exchange, students must have the permission of their academic advisers for exchange courses, the LRPC does not expect any serious problem of unqualified students in such courses. An increased number of exchange students from the University can be expected, especially when its honors program gets under way. However, for the time being there may continue to be some legitimate restraints on completely free exchange between the University and the colleges.

There are some less rational obstacles to cooperation between the colleges and the University which the Committee believes can be overcome by increased information and contact. Some faculty members at the colleges are still influenced by attitudes toward the University which stem from the time when one of the main advantages to the University from cooperation was that it could share some of the prestige of the colleges. These faculty members still think of the University as a small state institution, poorly supported financially, and just emerging from "Mass Aggie." There are other faculty members, however, who fear that as the University gets bigger and better, it will tend to absorb the colleges into its orbit, forgetting its "obligation" to the colleges for past services, and developing its programs and facilities without consultation.

The LRPC is aware of the legitimacy of this fear. This report stresses throughout that the maintenance of the diversity of the institutions is essential. The Committee does believe, however, that it is in the interest of the University as well as of the colleges to be an integral part of the cooperative program and that failure to accomplish this now will make it more difficult to accomplish in the future.

The LRPC also recognizes legitimate restraints on totally free exchange among the colleges. Each college offers an educational experience and environment different from that of the others, and makes somewhat different judgments concerning the suitability of any particular course for its own educational goals and program. This is not only inevitable but desirable.

The Committee believes, however, that some negative attitudes are related to lack of information and communication both within and among the institutions. Among many of the faculty there appears to be mistrust and fear of the purposes of cooperation, a suspicion that cooperation is a concept fostered by the Presidents of the institutions with the primary purpose of saving money. As a result, some individuals and departments fear cutbacks in staff and programs by consolidation of smaller or weaker departments or the dropping of programs which are not in great demand. Some faculty members with whom the Committee talked expressed concern about liberalizing regulations for exchange courses, for instance. If exchange were made completely free, the feeling went, what would happen to enrollment in the courses of a less popular teacher, or a stiffer grader, in competition with a better known teacher or an easier course at another institution? A few expressed the idea that such competition might improve teaching all around, but they were in the minority.

The recommendations in this report do not involve cutbacks of staff in established programs. They are intended to promote more efficient and coordinated use of existing staff and staff specialties and somewhat less expansion of staff to cover new programs and courses than would be necessary without cooperation. The Committee believes that this will be in the interest of all the institutions.

Planning cooperative programs among five institutions sometimes takes considerable time. This makes cooperation particularly difficult in any programs which one or more of the colleges consider to be urgent. No one wants to risk the possibility of having no program because a cooperative program did not work out, or could not be worked out rapidly. This was particularly apparent in recent discussions concerning Black Studies and programs for the disadvantaged—areas in which cooperation should be particularly fruitful because of their newness and the scarcity of funds and personnel. No foolproof answer for this problem exists, but the LRPC believes that some of the recommendations in this report concerning the governance of cooperation will help to solve it.

Several parts of the report point out that both faculty and students often cited difficulties of transportation, calendar, and scheduling as the major obstacles to cooperation. When the Committee tried to discover the specific problems, however, the grounds of the argument frequently shifted to problems of attitude and initiative. The Committee believes that if there were agreement that more must be done to facilitate interchange, and that coordination of calendar and schedule is important to this, such coordination would not pose insurmountable problems. If adequate transportation were viewed as crucial to a program universally desired, it would be assigned the necessary financial priorities. The dilemma is that many people think it is not worth the risk of putting large sums into improved transportation until the commitment to academic complementarity which would justify such expenditures is achieved, while others claim it is not feasible to develop academic complementarity until the transportation problem is solved. The problem must be attacked at one or another point. The LRPC believes that it would be helpful to eliminate the argument of inadequate transportation by an increase in funds rather than waiting for a change in faculty attitudes toward cooperation before this is done. We have, however, tried to recommend procedures which will accomplish both.

D. Principles of Cooperation

THE LRPC BELIEVES that it is important for all members of the five institutions to consider the kind of five-college cooperation they wish to achieve over the next ten or twenty years. The kind of cooperation the Committee proposes is spelled out more fully in the sections which follow. Here it is useful to summarize some basic principles.

First, the primary purpose of cooperation is to strengthen the educational programs of the institutions. Although relative financial savings might result from more efficient use of staff and facilities, cooperative programs are basically designed to help each institution do what it wishes to do but cannot accomplish, or cannot accomplish as well, within the limits of its own resources.

Second, cooperation cannot be imposed from the outside, but must be undertaken voluntarily, in recognition of mutual interests, by the individuals and groups on each campus who will be involved. This can occur if communication among these individuals and groups is improved. There has been a regrettable lack of information on all the campuses in the past about existing or potential cooperative projects and about the programs of each institution.

Third, it is important for each institution to preserve its individuality. Cooperation will be most effective if each institution is distinctive, if each has different strengths. Each might even agree, in consultation with the others, to work specifically toward building up particular strengths in advanced work, while maintaining the core of courses it considers necessary to maintain its identity and integrity as a liberal arts institution.

Fourth, maintaining institutional identity does not mean that each institution is entirely free to make its own plans without taking into account the possible effects of those plans on the other four. Institutional autonomy should be surrendered to the extent that each institution agrees to consult with the others before acting, while reserving to itself the ultimate power of decision.

Finally, it is important to recognize the indirect benefits as well as the direct benefits to be gained from five-college cooperation. The presence in the Valley of a variety of institutions has already helped to make each institution more attractive to both faculty and students. With increasing specialization of knowledge, it is becoming increasingly important for faculty and students to have the stimulus of contacts with a wider group of scholars than can be available on any one campus. More cooperative programs and better communication among the institutions can effect this.

E. The Valley Environment

AMHERST, SOUTH HADLEY, AND NORTHAMPTON, the three towns in which the colleges are located, and the town of Hadley, which is in the center of the five-college area and contiguous to the other towns, are very likely to grow substantially in population in the next few years. The major contributing factors are the growth of the University of Massachusetts, the creation of Hampshire College, the attractiveness of the area for residential development, the availability of land, increased accessibility from more heavily populated areas, and, of course, the pressure for living space from the general growth of population.

The environment of the five-college area is now relatively clean and pure. The sky seldom is palled with industrial or exhaust waste. Pure drinking water can still be found flowing in the springs and streams of surrounding hills. Green open land, uncurbed roads, dark country lanes, singing birds, swamps, forests, grazing cattle, and shade trees are characteristic of our environment. Sheer growth of population is a major threat to that environment because of its contribution to air and water pollution and to crowding and noise.

Although industrial development is unlikely to be a significant factor in the five-college area in the near future, commercialization will probably increase. The Amherst-

Hadley area is likely to become a major regional shopping center. The result will be increases in automobile traffic and more parking problems.

The increasing desire of students to control their own lives, together with the increasing costs and administrative problems for the colleges of providing student housing, make it likely that larger numbers of students will be permitted to live in non-college housing and will choose to do so. If the colleges greatly reduced their construction of additional housing units, substantial numbers of students would have to seek accommodations off campus. The results for the towns might be a severe testing of building, zoning, and occupancy codes, and a threat to the generally good town-gown relations for the five colleges and their home towns. A large number of students moving into housing not specifically designed for high density and student use, or into housing built for their use but with profit as the main motive, would have an immense impact on the environment. The effect, generally, would be an increase in the degenerative forces already at work in the five-college environment.

A possible development which may, on balance, contribute to the maintenance of the quality of the environment of the five-college area is the proposed Connecticut River National Recreation Area's Mount Holyoke unit. Legislation now before the Congress would establish in the Holyoke Range from Belchertown to Mount Tom and along the river a twelve-thousand-acre federally owned recreation area designed to preserve important ecological features, to protect the range in its natural state, and to provide on a permanent basis outdoor recreation opportunities such as hiking, camping, and skiing. Accompanying that development would be a concentrated effort to cleanse the Connecticut River of its present very heavy pollution so that the water would be acceptable for swimming. The plan includes proposals to allow farmers whose land might be in the area to continue farming as long as they wish, which would help to maintain the agricultural beauty of the Valley.

Although the creation of the National Recreation Area would protect from industrial and residential development a vast and important land area, it would also aggravate the problems of the towns surrounding the area because of the number of visitors the recreation area would attract. Service facilities such as shops, restaurants, gasoline stations, hostels, and marinas undoubtedly would be built to capitalize on the transient population. Such growth on the periphery of national parks and recreation areas is a well established phenomenon. In addition, there would be increasingly heavy traffic on the roads surrounding the area, on open fields in and out of the recreation area by snowmobiles and other cross-country vehicles, and on the river by motorboats, all of which disrupt balanced land use and contribute to water, air, and noise pollution.

In sum, then, the relatively high quality of the environment of the five colleges is likely to deteriorate rapidly in the years ahead. Population and traffic growth will result in more light, noise, pollution, inconvenience, dirt, and ugliness, with fewer trees and farms and less open space. The water and air are likely to be more polluted as commercial growth accelerates. Plant and animal life will gradually become less diversified as the ecology is modified. Certain plants and animals simply cannot survive; others will diminish in number.

What are the implications of such dire predictions for the five colleges? To a large extent the institutions and the residents of the area are trapped in a cycle of destructive change over which they have little control. The factors which could make for a better future are control of population growth, application of technology to problems of waste and pollution, and education in the problems of environmental quality. The five colleges should work with their communities to plan for the changes and to assist in making the development of the environment as orderly and civilized as possible.

F. Longer-Range Possibilities & Implications

The Long Range Planning Committee has made specific recommendations in this report only for a period in which operating conditions appear reasonably predictable. It has tried to take into account not only what is desirable but what is feasible for these particular institutions at this time. The recommendations for immediate action concern moves which we believe the faculties, students, and administrations could undertake now, and which we believe are essential to progress in cooperation. Other recommendations involve projects or policies which might need several years of study or preparatory activity.

But the Committee is aware that there are longer-range implications growing out of the immediate recommendations. While it has made no careful study of these, it has kept in mind a number of points which it thinks should be continuously examined during the years ahead.

The Committee believes that the primary long-range goal of five-college cooperation is the development of conscious complementarity among the institutions. Each institution should maintain its own integrity and identity, but it should recognize that its programs should complement rather than duplicate those of the others in all details. Some duplication, of course, is necessary and desirable. For new programs, however, and for highly specialized areas of study, cooperative planning and the development of different strengths can add to the resources of all at relatively less cost than would be incurred by each operating on its own. Such coordinated development, the Committee believes, might eventually be accomplished through something like a five-college educational policy committee, which would be responsible for reviewing proposals for new courses, programs, and faculty appointments within the framework of complementarity.

Within the next decade, calendars, course schedules, and

utilization of facilities may be designed for optimum student opportunity by computer analysis. Transportation from any one college to any other ideally should take not more than fifteen or twenty minutes. After more experience and analysis of the results of present experiments, student exchange among the five institutions on a semester or year basis with residential privileges might be permitted.

Certain services may also be centralized for maximum effectiveness. For instance, an admissions information, reference, and candidate exchange program might be created to assist student applicants to any one of the colleges to find an appropriate location and to help the colleges find the students they want. One business office and administrative computer might process and prepare financial records for the private colleges. Some service and buildings and grounds activities might be contracted centrally for the private colleges, or there might be a five-college pool of special service equipment.

These procedures, which the Committee recognizes as future rather than immediate possibilities, would not make of the five institutions one "multiversity" with five campuses, nor are they intended to create a sixth operating institution to which the other five would be subservient. Five Colleges, Inc., should continue to exist for the purpose of serving the five institutions, and should remain under their control.

However, the real benefits of cooperation, academic and financial, will come only as the five institutions begin to regard cooperation as central to their concerns, and as they develop methods of moving toward a conscious, though limited, complementarity.

I

Academic Complementarity

THE UNDERLYING IDEA of cooperation is the achievement of academic complementarity leading to mutual advantage: the offering of the strengths of one's own institution in return for access to the strengths of others. Each institution hopes to draw upon students, faculty, facilities, and resources at the other institutions that differ from and complement its own. The aim is to secure access to these additional resources without sacrificing the coherence of each institution or the integrity of its curricular programs.

The educational goal of the four undergraduate colleges and of the College of Arts and Sciences of the University is to provide a liberal arts education combining breadth of subject matter with analytical depth. Given this similarity of essential purpose, there will clearly be a necessary duplication and overlap in the course offerings central to a liberal arts curriculum. This basic similarity points to the importance of cooperative academic arrangements covering subjects that can enrich the central core of the liberal arts. It points also to the possibility of confidence among the institutions in each other's educational style and aim. For academic cooperation to yield its greatest benefits, faculties must have detailed knowledge of and confidence in each other. We are fortunate in the Valley that this knowledge and confidence are increasing.

In this section of the report we set out a variety of possible forms that cooperation may take. There is no single model for cooperative activity; different forms are best suited to different purposes. Every academic program that may benefit from cooperation requires that thought be given to the best mode or form for it. Both the analytical possibilities and past or present examples are examined here.

Many reasons why academic cooperation is desirable are suggested throughout the body of this report. The most obvious opportunities can be mentioned at the outset by way of illustration: the sharing of highly specialized and scarce faculty members whose specialties are important to the curricula of two or more colleges; the use of specialized facilities or collections to maximum benefit; the avoidance of duplication in offerings when demand is small; the introduction of new fields of knowledge with greater speed and with less competitive bidding than might otherwise be possible; the provision of coeducation in at least such fields as film and dramatic arts, where the participation of both sexes may be at times essential.

A. Faculty Exchange

Individual Arrangements

The term "faculty exchange" designates any arrangement by which a faculty member teaches on more than one campus. In the past, exchanges have usually served to fill a temporary gap in one of the faculties resulting from a leave of absence, an unexpected resignation, an unexpectedly large enrollment in a course, or an inability to hire a faculty member to fill a particular vacancy. Willingness of each college to allow its faculty members to help out on such occasions provides valuable assistance to all of the institutions.

Faculty exchange is also used to provide instruction in areas of the curriculum that are in such small demand that it is not feasible to have a full range of teaching skills on each campus, and in areas involving rare skills. To have a faculty member, rather than students, travel from one campus to another makes particularly good sense when there are substantial numbers of students to be taught on each campus.

Faculty exchange may also serve the professional interest of the faculty member himself. Some faculty members find positive values in teaching on another campus, such as the opportunity to meet colleagues, to teach men or women if they are located at one of the noncoeducational institutions, and especially to teach graduate students if they do not have that opportunity at their home campus. Teaching on more than one campus also may offer the possibility of more concentrated specialization than would be possible as a member of a small department on one of the college campuses.

Arrangements for faculty exchange can be worked out in a variety of ways. The most common form of faculty exchange has been overtime borrowing. Under this plan, a faculty member with the permission of his home institution teaches a course at another institution in addition to his normal program at home. For this he is paid according to his rank at a schedule of rates agreed upon by the five Presidents.

In a few cases, colleges have traded faculty members for one course in a semester. Each is released from one course on his own campus in order to teach a course on the other campus. No exchange of funds between individuals or institutions takes place. The administrative simplicity of this arrangement, once a desirable complementarity of teaching skills has been found, commends it as a method of faculty exchange to be exploited more in the future than it has been.

A second form of released-time faculty exchange involves a single faculty member who is released from one course by his home institution to teach elsewhere. In this case, the borrowing institution pays to the home institution a proportionate share of the individual's regular compensation. This form of released-time borrowing has occurred when two institutions agreed to share for a period of years the services of an individual who holds his appointment in one of them.

A matter that merits further study is the extent to which it may be possible and desirable for a department at the University to work out an arrangement with one or more college departments permitting some faculty members recruited for the college departments to come to the Valley with the understanding at the outset that they would have an opportunity to participate in some graduate teaching. Not all the colleges may consider this appropriate for their own recruiting; in some quarters the view is held that faculty members at a college should normally be fully committed to undergraduate teaching. This is probably one of the areas in which cooperation need not be parallel: each college could formulate its own policy.

From time to time corresponding departments of two or more institutions have agreed to offer a course cooperatively, usually with faculty members from more than one institution joining in giving a course to a combined group of students. Such a course is usually listed in the offerings of each institution, though the meetings might be held on another campus or might move from one campus to another during the semester. The faculty member involved receives credit for the course in the normal teaching load at home. This arrangement closely resembles the interdepartmental course given on a single campus in which faculty members of more than one department receive teaching credit.

Occasions also arise in which an institution wishes to have the assistance of a faculty member from another college not for a whole course, but for a few lectures or other portion of the course. In such instances, what amounts to part-time overtime borrowing can occur. There is no set schedule of rates covering such part-time borrowing, but up to now this has been sufficiently infrequent and informal not to present a problem. Faculty members have also served on other campuses as outside examiners in graduate programs, honors programs, or comprehensive examination programs. Sometimes a fee is paid for this; sometimes, as in the case of any college faculty member who is a member of the graduate faculty at the University but is not currently teaching a course, there is no fee. In the latter case, the individual has no formal obligation to serve, but may be willing to do so because he wants to maintain some connection with the graduate teaching program.

Related to individual faculty exchange, though perhaps not technically part of it, is the use by one college of a graduate assistant who is enrolled as a student at one of the other institutions. This has not been a common occurrence, but is a possibility to be explored more fully, particularly as the colleges find it increasingly necessary to make the most efficient possible use of the funds available to them for instructional salaries. Properly supervised, graduate assistants constitute a potential pool of help for the colleges, and may themselves find benefits in the opportunity to teach on a smaller campus.

It is clear that faculty exchange is intimately part of the broader subject of academic cooperation. Faculty exchange in the past has served chiefly to help institutions in staffing emergencies and to provide for faculty members a greater variety in teaching or additional income. As a way of enriching the curriculum and of allowing more efficient use of resources through advanced planning, faculty exchange has not, in the opinion of the LRPC, been fully exploited. Although an institution can be expected to need most of the teaching time of the faculty members it has recruited, willingness to share from time to time, occasionally even at some inconvenience, would be a reasonable price to pay for the reciprocal benefits.

The LRPC suggests that faculty exchange be a subject for continuing study by departments and by the Five College Academic Policy Advisory Council proposed later in this report. Released-time borrowing rather than overtime borrowing should be encouraged whenever possible to minimize dilution of the quality of teaching. The possibility of offering graduate teaching as a part of the regular duties of some college faculty members should be explored by the University and any of the colleges that would like such an option.

Institutional Arrangements

In addition to an arrangement that enables an individual to teach on another campus, cooperative academic programs may evolve that have more permanent, structural consequences for the institutions. The joint department, with a single chairman based at one of the institutions and with members of the department based at other institutions, is the clearest example of such an arrangement. The Astronomy Department is now organized in this fashion.

Other possible ways of coordinated academic planning among five institutions are: 1) separate departments on each campus, with introductory work offered on each campus and advanced work, coordinated to avoid duplication, offered on several; 2) separate departments on several campuses, with introductory work available on each but much of the advanced work done at a single institution; 3) a strong department on one campus, where a student would take the majority of both introductory and advanced courses, but with related courses available on other campuses; 4) special undergraduate programs on several campuses, with coordination among the programs and a graduate department with specialized faculty at the University.

These possible cooperative arrangements may be strengthened through faculty exchange, joint appointments, and visiting appointments. That is, individual arrangements may be used to buttress institutional arrangements. But it is clear that cooperative academic planning built upon a joint department or upon the coordinated work of departments at two or more institutions requires long-term commitment and continued administrative support in a way not required for individual arrangements. To sustain institutional academic cooperation, educational policy committees, Deans, and department chairmen must be cognizant of the possible consequences of their own actions to other institutions.

A variety of cooperative academic activities involving institutional arrangements are discussed below. Before beginning this more detailed presentation, it is important to note some of the requirements for cooperative planning.

B. Requirements for Cooperative Planning

Information: Inventories and Catalogues

In the course of its work during the year, the LRPC has become aware of the clear need for more accurate and adequate information about faculty specialties and course offerings in a form that can readily be shared among the five institutions. Early in its deliberations the Committee agreed that the collection of statistics on faculty staffing, course offerings, and student enrollments is essential. Of particular importance is information about scholarly interests, competencies, and experience that may contribute to coordinated planning for special programs such as area studies. The Committee's sense of need for such an inventory led to a proposal to expand the currently used personnel information systems of the University of Massachusetts to include additional items and then to extend collection procedures to the other institutions in the Valley. The LRPC recommends that such an inventory of faculty resources on a continuing basis be prepared as soon as possible.

The Committee found that the second major category of information that would be most useful is the equivalent of a five-college catalogue. Pasteups of the present catalogues prepared by Hampshire College for the social sciences and the natural sciences are both useful and illuminating. Putting the catalogue offerings side by side reveals graphically the heavy areas of duplication in certain disciplines as well as areas touched upon by only one or two courses at all the institutions together or not covered at all. A committee should be assigned to recommend ways of coordinating the five course catalogues.

One possibility might be to print overruns on the normal order of each college catalogue, and to make these available in loose-leaf form for insertion into ring binders. Another method, already used by several departments, is to prepare mimeographed lists for each discipline that would serve as an index to the full catalogues. To be useful, these lists should be available at the time of preregistration on each campus for courses during the following semester.

A third possible method would be to have each department at each institution include at the end of its section of the course catalogue a listing, by course number and title only, of all courses given by the comparable departments at the other institutions which do not duplicate its own offerings. Each department could be requested to send listings of its offerings to the other departments no later than a certain date each year (say, a month in advance of the earliest deadline for the submission of catalogue material), and those responsible for the compilation of the course catalogues could be instructed not to accept any departmental listings which do not include listings of courses at the other institutions. Courses at one institution which do not fall within the listings of any department at another could be included in separate listings by those in general charge of preparing the catalogues. This procedure would make information on courses at the other institutions readily available to both students and advisers. Once alerted by the listing in the home catalogue, they could easily find fuller course descriptions in the catalogues of the other institutions.

This procedure, though it would present some problems, should not be unduly time consuming for departments and would be relatively inexpensive. The additional course listings could be printed in small type and thus would add relatively few pages to each catalogue.

A third category of shared information which the Committee believes is needed is a union list of library holdings. The many problems connected with the creation of a union catalogue are discussed in Section VIII. E. A beginning was made by a proposal for a union serials list to be compiled and distributed by the facilities of the University of Massachusetts, for which the five colleges would share the cost. This proposal has been approved by the five Presidents, and distribution of a union serials list to all five-college faculty members is anticipated for the fall of 1969. The Committee strongly recommends that the publication of this joint serials list become a permanent service.

Institutional Self-Discipline

Faculty exchange, coordinated programs, and planned academic cooperation will come about less as a result of efforts focused in the first instance directly on cooperation than as a result of the careful analysis and subsequent rationalization of the course offerings of the several institutions. A necessary first step is that faculty members from different campuses become more knowledgeable about each other's teaching interests and, therefore, better able to coordinate course offerings in a complementary fashion. There will continue to be many instances where duplication, or near duplication, should continue; there will be instances where faculty members or departments, even though fully informed of five-college resources, choose for sound reasons to duplicate courses or facilities that already exist at another campus. The concern of the LRPC is first and foremost that such decisions be made with full information available and in the light of possible actions to be taken at other institutions and possible consequences of the action of one's own institution upon the others.

The necessary self-discipline must be exercised early enough in the formulation of educational policy within each institution to permit adjustments and alterations to reflect five-college considerations. Such a procedure requires much better and more regular consultation than now exists. Each institution has a body which authorizes the introduction of new courses and programs. The LRPC recommends that any proposal to that body for a significantly new course or instructional program by a department, interdepartmental group, school, or other teaching entity at any of the five institutions be required to include a statement setting forth the relationship between the proposed offering and the offerings of the other institutions. If the proposed offering involves overlapping or duplication of other offerings in the Valley, the reasons for introducing it nonetheless should be clearly stated. The LRPC recognizes that in many instances the legitimacy and necessity of duplication will be so apparent that the reasons for it can be stated briefly. If the proposed offering does not duplicate or overlap, the proposal should indicate that the projected course or program has been discussed with appropriate persons at the other institutions to ascertain whether similar new offerings are being considered on more than one campus and that the appropriateness of a jointly-sponsored offering has been at least considered.

The principle that major decisions within each institution should explicitly take account of five-college possibilities has its counterpart in the LRPC's belief that there should be developed a means for ensuring that recommendations of official five-college committees receive serious attention in each institution. Accordingly, the LRPC proposes that when a given institution decides not to act in accordance with the formal recommendation of an official five-college committee, the President should inform the other institutions and the Coordinator of the decision and of the reasons for it.

C. A Five College Academic Policy Advisory Council

Although direct consultation between departments and individual faculty members of the five colleges is basic to effective academic cooperation, a necessary adjunct to the self-discipline of departments, committees, and Deans is a regular central channel for discussion of academic matters among the institutions. The LRPC therefore recommends the establishment of a Five College Academic Policy Advisory Council (APAC). This Council would include a faculty member representing the chief educational policy committee of each institution, a student from each institution chosen from the senior academic committee on which students serve, and the Deputy from each institution.

The Council would receive reports from interdisciplinary councils and from such other five-college academic groups or committees as are in continuous existence. It would also initiate inquiry into other aspects of curricular activity where cooperation may from time to time offer promise of increased resources, flexibility of offerings, and strengthened programs. For this purpose it might create ad hoc study committees or propose the establishment of new continuing committees to deal with new cooperative academic activities. In addition, the Council would review the effectiveness of measures designed to increase the flow of academic information among the campuses, for example the cross listing of courses in catalogues suggested above, and would recommend such new or improved procedures as it might think desirable.

The Council would be responsible for seeing that the academic policy committee of each institution is kept informed of the others' discussions and activities, especially where they may affect five-college cooperation. It would report after each of its regular meetings to the President of each institution or to the person designated by the President to receive its reports.

RECOMMENDATIONS

1. Improvement in the system of faculty exchange among the five colleges should be a subject for continuing study by departments and by the Five College Academic Policy Advisory Council. Released-time borrowing rather than overtime borrowing should be encouraged. The possibility of offering graduate teaching as a part of the regular duties of some college faculty members should be explored by the University and any of the colleges that would like such an option.
2. Exchange of information among the five colleges should be substantially increased. An inventory of faculty resources should be developed and published on an annual basis. A means should be found for making more readily available to all students and faculty members in the Valley information on the course offerings of all the institutions.
3. Each of the five institutions should accept the principle, and find means for ensuring, that any proposal for a new course, instructional program, or major facility include a statement setting forth the relationship between it and the offerings of the other institutions, with explicit discussion of the possibilities of five-college cooperation and the reasons for proceeding either cooperatively or unilaterally.
4. If one institution decides not to act in accordance with the advice or recommendations of an official five-college committee, the President should, in writing, inform the other institutions and the Coordinator of the decision and of the reasons for it.
5. A Five College Academic Policy Advisory Council (APAC) should be established, to include from

each institution a faculty member representing the chief educational policy committee, a student chosen from the senior academic committee on which students serve, and the five-college Deputy. All five-college academic committees and councils should report to APAC.

II

Cooperative Academic Programs & Activities

A. Interdisciplinary Studies & Councils

SEVERAL PRESENT academic programs in the Valley, and others still in the planning stage, require the participation of faculty members representing various disciplines. The essentially interdisciplinary nature of geographic area studies, or of Black or Urban Studies, suggests both the need for interdepartmental cooperation within each institution and the advantages of institutional cooperation among the five colleges. Programs of such scope require a wide range of highly specialized skills, which are seldom available on a single campus. Haphazard development of such interdisciplinary programs of study or the attempt of a single institution to evolve these programs by itself is likely to lead to those duplications, imbalances, and omissions which complementary planning might prevent.

Because the special programs discussed in this section may so clearly derive strength from institutional cooperation, the Long Range Planning Committee recommends below the establishment of a number of interdisciplinary Councils. The Councils are recommended for several geographic area programs, as well as for Black Studies and Urban Studies. Three Councils in the arts, one for performing arts, one for fine arts, and one for film, are also proposed.

The Councils would be advisory groups, calling to the attention of the Five College Academic Policy Advisory Council the desirability of particular cooperative actions with respect to the study of a given area—whether the action be to hire someone with a particular competency, to offer a new course somewhere in the Valley, to buy a certain collection or series of materials, to develop an overseas program, or to provide a forum where interested faculty members and students could discuss their views. APAC might in turn initiate proposals, recommending to one of the interdisciplinary Councils that it consider a particular course of action and asking an evaluation of its merits.

The LRPC does not recommend a single procedure for establishing all the Councils but suggests only that each be constituted of faculty members and students drawn from a variety of disciplines whose special interest and competency centers on the particular area; that procedures be defined for the early selection of a Chairman; that the Councils meet regularly; and that they report their recommendations to the Academic Policy Advisory Council.

1. GEOGRAPHIC AREA STUDIES

In the sections which follow, we attempt to describe the present status of and the future prospects for the study of six different geographic areas. Substantial library holdings already exist in the Valley and there are a number of faculty specialists in the disciplines bearing upon each of these areas. Cooperative activities among geographic area specialists in the colleges and University have been sustained at least since 1959, when the four institutions were given the first of two Ford Foundation grants, totaling over half a million dollars, for a cooperative Asian-African Studies program. The Five College Faculty Seminar on Latin America and the Seminar on Communism are examples of current arrangements for the exchange of ideas among those interested in a particular region.

With the expiration of the Ford Foundation grant in the summer of 1968, the Asian and African Studies Committee charged with oversight of the program looked to the future of international studies in the Valley. In its report to the five college Presidents the Committee expressed the view

> that the role of Asian and African studies in the Valley should now be redefined. To that end, it suggests to the Presidents . . . that a new body with new terms of reference be constituted. As long-range cooperative plans are being considered, this seems an opportune time for a reassessment and a strengthening of Asian and African studies (and indeed international studies as a whole) in the liberal arts curriculum.

The LRPC's survey of the current agencies and activities in the five colleges which bring together geographic area specialists has led to the view that while these are rewarding for those who participate and while they have fostered institutional cooperation, they serve only incidentally the purpose of complementary academic planning.

To foster complementary academic planning, certain Geographic Area Councils should be created. In the discussion of the particular areas which follow, specific topics are suggested as of special importance for a Council's consideration. Other topics will doubtless emerge during the early discussions of the Councils.

Decisions concerning the kinds and nature of foreign language instruction essential to the study of a geographic area clearly should follow discussions by each Area Council. Cooperative planning is especially important here to avoid unnecessary duplication in the hiring of teachers of esoteric languages, and to provide for students in the Valley the opportunity to study on at least one of the five campuses a language indispensable to the understanding of a given region. Arabic, Hindi, and Urdu, for example, are not now available to students of the Middle East and India. Studies of these areas and library resources supporting them will be handicapped until these languages are introduced. The identification of such needs and of potential duplications in the five-college foreign language offerings should be a central concern of the Councils.

RECOMMENDATION

Geographic Area Councils, constituted of faculty and student representatives of each of the five institutions, should be established for the areas of the Soviet Union and Eastern Europe, Latin America, East Asia, South and Southeast Asia, and the Middle East. These Councils should take as their explicit aim the achievement of complementary resources in faculty, library, and curriculum among the five colleges.

a. Soviet Union & Eastern Europe

Formal cooperation of faculty from the four institutions that offer courses dealing with Russia began only in 1965 and is still largely limited to the Faculty Seminar on Communism. Since its inception in 1965, this seminar has met monthly in the Smith Faculty Center. At each meeting a speaker has been brought in from outside the area, usually a faculty member from an institution such as Columbia, Harvard, or Michigan, though on a few occasions a speaker has been drawn from the United States government or a foreign government. Almost all speakers have presented the results of recent or continuing research. Until last year the seminar was funded by Smith College. In 1968–69 the Government Department of the University paid the fees of two speakers. Two faculty members from Amherst and one from Mount Holyoke attend regularly; the average attendance at the meetings has been about fifteen. Through this limited means faculty members have come to know one another, to learn about one another's research, and to discuss common interests. Occasionally seminar members have invited additional faculty members with a peripheral interest in this area to hear and meet with speakers on subjects of direct interest to them. In addition, some participation by faculty members in courses at institutions other than their own has occurred, but this has been quite limited.

Although the seminar has indirectly encouraged the development of resources for work in the area, much remains to be done both on an individual institutional and on a cooperative basis. The University and Smith have more extensive programs in Russian and East European Studies than Amherst and Mount Holyoke, and thus employ a majority of the faculty involved in courses on Russia. The total number of faculty members involved in Russian and East European Studies in the Valley exceeds that of any other single area studies group. Smith has very good library holdings, particularly in Russian literature. In total materials the University collection has recently surpassed that at Smith, at least in acquisitions dated from 1966 onwards. The University library now has a collection of between ten and twenty thousand volumes on Russia and Eastern Europe. The University's interest in this area is important to all students of Soviet and Eastern European Studies in the Valley: a Slavic bibliographer has been appointed to the library staff and he has greatly improved the basic collection in two years, and the library staff is working on a rapidly growing collection of materials in the Eastern European languages. It is unlikely that the libraries of the other three institutions will acquire such materials, nor will they need to if cooperative relations continue to develop in both program and library resources.

At present, four-college cooperation in Russian Studies is at a point from which it may develop on a broader basis in several ways. Recently a Soviet and East European Studies Group was formed at the University, which will probably establish an undergraduate program in Russian and East European Studies, an interdisciplinary course, and a faculty seminar. Although the group at present includes only about twenty-five faculty members, all within the College of Arts and Sciences, it is likely that it will come to include faculty from other schools, such as the School of Business and the College of Agriculture. Ultimately the group hopes to aid in the establishment of formal five-college undergraduate and graduate programs in which a certificate in Russian and East European Studies would be awarded. At present this program is not visualized as an interdisciplinary degree, but only as a concentration in the area study, with the degree requirements in one of the established disciplines still being met. The group also anticipates the enlargement of the faculty seminar now meeting at Smith (to which only a limited number of non-Smith faculty could heretofore be invited); the establishment of a five-college interdisciplinary course on Russia and/or Eastern Europe; and the creation of a five-college study-travel session abroad, perhaps in Munich, Vienna, or even the U.S.S.R., on the model of those sponsored by Oberlin, Kansas, Oklahoma, and other American colleges and universities. The necessity for financial support is a major factor in the implementation of these plans. The group is already involved in discussing a combination of support from the five colleges, foundations, and perhaps the United States government.

If the program cannot be realized as a five-college venture the group will attempt to establish it as a University program, at least in its basic form as an undergraduate certificate program, an interdisciplinary course, and a faculty seminar.

During 1968–69 an informal five-college faculty-student group met on several occasions to exchange information on courses in Slavic Studies and to consider ways of coordinating relevant lectures and cultural events.

The LRPC recommends that a Russian and East European Studies Council give consideration not only to the larger and more general questions enunciated in the prefatory discussion of interdisciplinary Councils but also to the particular questions of the development of an interdisciplinary undergraduate seminar in Russian and East European Studies and the establishment of a cooperative undergraduate program leading to the awarding of a certificate in Russian and East European Studies.

b. Latin America

Four-college cooperative activities in the field of Latin American Studies have increased steadily since 1964, when a joint listing of relevant courses was initiated, designed primarily to assist students of Latin America in planning their programs. Approximately fifty courses, some dealing exclusively with Latin America and some more general courses on related topics, appear in the four-college list for 1968–69. They include courses offered by departments of art, anthropology, sociology, biology, economics, geography, government or political science, history, and literature.

In 1965, a four-college interdisciplinary Faculty Seminar on Latin America was begun with funds supplied by the four institutions. The seminar has now completed its third year of regular meetings. Meetings held about once a month enable members to discuss their own current research on Latin American topics and to hear papers from distinguished outside scholars. Approximately twenty Latin American specialists, or faculty members with an interest in Latin America, attend each meeting, and the seminar mailing list numbers fifty-five to sixty faculty members and administrators of the Valley colleges. Of those who participate actively in the seminar, six or seven are drawn from Amherst, Smith, and Mount Holyoke; the majority are from the University of Massachusetts. The meetings rotate among the colleges.

This faculty seminar was of interest to the LRPC, since it is the major device for interinstitutional activity in the field of Latin American Studies. The seminar has often been cited in support of the belief that Latin American Studies has been one of the most successful models of cooperative organization and exchange in the Valley.

Our findings confirm that the seminar has indeed been useful to its members, not only for the sharing of their academic interests in Latin America, but as a means of getting to know neighboring faculty and the courses they teach. Participants report that the knowledge thus gained has proved useful in advising exchange students and has resulted in considerable consultation and coordination in terms of course offerings and faculty hirings. Yet these claims for effective communication and coordination, justified perhaps when viewed in relation to present cooperative practices in other fields, are sharply qualified by several Latin Americanists, who find cooperation in this area to be haphazard and inefficient and believe that no real effort has been made to achieve a coherent program which avoids duplication in hiring and courses.

Recommendations from Latin Americanists concerning what might be done to achieve effective cooperation range from general proposals for complete reorganization of all area studies programs to detailed programs of special seminars and symposia. The central theme of these recommendations is the need to provide students—not only faculty—with opportunities for sustained inquiry and discussion. The LRPC is convinced that student interest in the underdeveloped nations, specifically in Latin America as the Western "Third World," will continue to grow, and that this interest derives from a sound judgment of political realities. There is increasing interest in permitting concentrations which are not bound to the requirements of conventional departmental majors. Mount Holyoke now offers a major in Latin American Studies, for example; Smith offers a major in Hispanic-American Studies; and the University offers a certificate in Latin American Studies within a disciplinary major. Some thought has already been given to the possibility of a five-college certificate program in Latin American Studies at both the undergraduate and graduate levels.

The present Latin American Faculty Seminar provides occasion for regular meetings of area scholars, but it is not designed, nor should it be, as a cooperative program-planning agency. The LRPC therefore recommends the formation of a Latin American Studies Council to explore the possibilities of more effective cooperation in this area.

c. East Asia

Circumstances suggest that East Asian Studies in the Valley should prosper. Although no one of the colleges can claim an adequate and balanced program of East Asian Studies, the course offerings of the five colleges as a whole provide a wide range of opportunities for the student of China and Japan—Asian demography, for example, at Mount Holyoke; Chinese and Japanese language study at Smith and the University respectively; Japanese history at Amherst; Oriental philosophy and religion at all four institutions; contemporary Chinese government and politics at Smith and at the University; Japanese demography and Far Eastern anthropology at the University; Japanese and Chinese art at Mount Holyoke and Smith. Among the forty courses in Asian-African Studies offered at all the Valley institutions in the spring semester of 1969, twenty-four were concerned in whole or in part with China and/or Japan. Opportunities for study abroad are provided through Smith's program in the Philippines, Amherst's relationship with Doshisha University in Japan, and the University's relationship with Hokkaido University in Sapporo, Japan.

The University is now moving decisively toward a strengthening of its undergraduate East Asia program, and to this end has appointed for 1969–70 a new chairman of its program of Asian Studies. The new chairman, a Japanese language and literature scholar, has declared his intention of building a strong language program; the University may eventually have a Department of Asian Languages. Hampshire College is exploring the feasibility of Chinese language instruction in its summer Language Institutes, as well as considering the contribution it might make to Chinese area studies in the Valley. Though at least three East Asian scholars will soon leave the Valley or retire, it seems clear that a net increase of faculty in East Asian languages and culture is in the making.

The testimony of present faculty in this area indicates a growing student interest in East Asia. The one teacher of the Chinese language among the five colleges finds himself with an increasing number of students; the University's appointment for 1969–70 of a scholar in Chinese language and literature will bring him needed relief. Two professors, of East Asian government and history, report that their class enrollments have steadily increased; one reports that his freshman and sophomore students have proposed an Asian Studies major. This is consistent with evidence elsewhere in the nation of students' growing concern with the "Third World."

A few years ago the University established a Seminar in Asian Studies, designed to bring together scholars (mainly from the University) to share their ideas. The lapse of the seminar has been attributed to the diversity of its members' interests, a natural consequence of the diversity of the geographic areas which constitute Asia; interests were not as shared as had been hoped. This suggests the wisdom of establishing a more narrowly defined Area Council, which would take for its area China, Japan, and Korea, that is, a Council on East Asian Studies. Thus, while we find ourselves in general agreement with the recommendations for cooperative planning contained in the final Report to the Presidents by the Asian and African Studies Committee (June 28, 1968), we propose that the tasks recommended in that report for assignment to a single Asian-African Committee should be the work of several Councils, one of them representative of East Asian Studies only. The East Asian Studies Council should concern itself with a search for faculty with competencies now absent in the five-college program; the development of a coordinated policy for library acquisitions and a considerable strengthening of East Asian library holdings, which are not now sufficient to attract faculty in Asian

Studies to the Valley; and the development of additional openings for students in overseas programs, perhaps through arrangements with Taiwan National University and/or with the Chinese University of Hong Kong.

d. South and Southeast Asia

The Ford Foundation grant for African and Asian Studies helped the colleges and the University to develop both course work and library resources in the areas of South and Southeast Asia. Smith offers courses in the area in both government and economics; Mount Holyoke and the University have courses in Southeast Asian politics and development; and the University has specialists in Indian and Southeast Asian sociology, anthropology and philosophy. However, there is no historian of the area in any of the institutions, and some of the courses noted above are offered only intermittently. The programs for this area are therefore weaker than for most other geographic areas.

There have been lecture series supported by the Ford Foundation grant, and South and Southeast Asia have been treated in interdisciplinary faculty seminars on political and economic development. The Ford Foundation grant also supported the expansion of library resources at all of the colleges and in the Hampshire Inter-Library Center, but area specialists believe that the collections for Southeast Asia, particularly, still need to be strengthened.

A South and Southeast Asia Studies Council should consider especially the appointment of an area historian to one of the five faculties and the augmentation of library resources, particularly for Southeast Asia.

e. Middle East

Middle East Studies in the four colleges essentially began with history courses offered at Amherst, Mount Holyoke, and Smith from the late 1950's on. In 1960–61 a further step was taken when the Ford Foundation grant permitted the four colleges to engage the assistance of the Harvard Center for Middle Eastern Studies. Members of the Harvard Center lectured weekly, and one offered seminars to develop and reinforce material presented in the lectures. At about this time, other departments began to take more extensive note of the Middle East in their course offerings. The Ford Foundation grant also included sums for library acquisitions, and thanks largely to this impetus, the Valley colleges began to build a collection which is now substantial in secondary materials and in Arabic, Persian, and Turkish materials in translation. In recent years the University has continued and expanded this nuclear collection.

A survey of present course offerings shows that Amherst and Smith offer the widest variety and the greatest depth in a number of departments. History is still the strongest of the disciplines represented. Recent developments include the introduction of a general survey of Islamic history as well as a specialized course on the Ottoman Empire at the University; the addition of an Islamist to the Religion Department at Mount Holyoke; the engagement of a visiting lecturer in Islamic Religion at Smith, to be shared with Amherst; and the introduction of a course on Eastern Christianity at Smith.

During 1968–69 a group of Valley scholars with a common interest in the Middle East met occasionally for dinner and discussions. These meetings were very successful, and it has been proposed that they continue next year on a more formal and regular basis, with scholarly papers invited from faculty members within and beyond the Valley.

Such meetings, like those of the Latin Americanists, are primarily designed to provide for the exchange of ideas pertaining to a particular geographic area and the sharing of common research interests. Seminars or colloquia for faculty and students of a given region should be encouraged. But the LRPC believes that a Middle East Studies Council would serve the crucial additional role of bringing Middle

East scholars together for the explicit purpose of complementary academic planning for the five institutions. The LRPC recommends to the attention of such a Council the addition of an expert in the Arabic language to the faculty of one of the Valley institutions who would offer not only introductory and intermediate Arabic, but also, eventually, advanced courses in the language; the addition of a sociologist or an anthropologist specializing in Middle East Studies to one of the institutions; the organization of a seminar group drawn from the Valley institutions to encourage research and the exchange of ideas; and consideration by the libraries of acquisitions of Arabic texts once language instruction becomes available.

f. Africa

The original Ford Foundation grant for Asian and African Studies at the four colleges was directed in substantial part to building the resources for African Studies. Library resources at each institution and at the Hampshire Inter-Library Center were augmented. New courses were introduced, particularly in the disciplines of anthropology, history, and political science. Systematic attention to African arts and literature in the Valley, however, came only slowly and sporadically.

African Studies now commands a vast literature in many disciplines and there exist rigorous graduate programs at many institutions, both in the United States and abroad. The LRPC considered recommending the establishment of an African Studies Council similar to those proposed for other geographic areas. It should be possible to establish such a council if interest develops. For the present, however, the LRPC has chosen in this report to link Africa with the Caribbean and North America under the heading Black Studies and to suggest a single Black Studies Council. The shortage of faculty and the nature of student interest suggest such an arrangement. Furthermore, putting emphasis upon the historic interconnections of the black experience on both sides of the Atlantic results in comparisons of general significance in method and in substance.

African scholars, particularly those interested in the eastern and northern parts of the continent, have reason as well to keep informed of current developments in Islamic studies. Students and scholars of Africa may wish, therefore, to participate in the activities of the Middle East Studies Council as well as of the Black Studies Council.

2. BLACK STUDIES

Each of the five colleges is considering or has already decided to institute some sort of academic program under the general heading "Black Studies" or "Afro-American Studies." A five-college approach to Black Studies has been suggested by black students and faculty members in the Valley. In the spring of 1969, a group which called itself the Ad Hoc Advisory Committee for the Five College Program of Black Studies proposed the establishment of a program in each institution and also the appointment of a Director of a five-college Black Studies program. The Long Range Planning Committee agrees that this is an area in which five-college cooperation is desirable and necessary.

Black Studies programs may be organized in a variety of ways. They may focus on Afro-American culture—the black experience in American history, the social and cultural contributions of black men and women in the United States and elsewhere, and the role of black Americans in contemporary American political and social developments. Or Black Studies can be conceived to involve primarily the history and cultures of peoples of African descent in Africa, the Caribbean, and the Americas, including comparative analyses of slavery and its consequences for cultural survival and the study of black self-assertion on both sides of the Atlantic since World War II. These two possible approaches are interrelated. It may be that one of the essential themes of Black Studies is also a tension within it: to what extent is the linking of African and Caribbean cultures and histories with the culture and history of black Americans intellectually justifiable? The question may present both an organizing assumption and a central issue for study. In any event, many disciplines must be brought to bear on Black Studies, although primary emphasis will be given to anthropology and sociology, history, the arts (including dance), oral and written literature, religion, and politics.

It was clear to the Committee that it is difficult to find people with the necessary training and skills to teach in the area of Black Studies. Such teachers may be highly specialized, and a carefully constructed program requires the coordination of a number of disciplines. The four operating institutions also have significant materials and facilities which might well be shared. Considerable use was made of the original Ford Foundation grant to buy books on Africa for the four college libraries and for HILC. African periodical and newspaper holdings in the Valley libraries are diverse. Each college has introduced courses on the black experience in America, black literature, and minority politics. Each campus, in association with its Afro-American Society, either now has or soon will have a Black Culture Center or Afro-American Center. For all these reasons, Black Studies seems a particularly appropriate area for five-college cooperation.

In keeping with the recommendations on foreign Area Studies Councils, the LRPC proposes the creation of a Black Studies Council that would include the directors of the undergraduate programs at all the institutions and other faculty members whose primary teaching duties or research interests are concerned with African, Caribbean, and black American themes. An active Black Studies Council could assist significantly in the planning of complementary curricular offerings, in the recruiting of additional professional staff, and in the coordinated provision of books, tapes, films, slides, and a variety of other resources necessary for the teaching of the subject.

RECOMMENDATION

A Black Studies Council composed of faculty and student representatives of each institution should be established to advance the creation and coordination of Black Studies courses and programs.

3. URBAN STUDIES

Urban Studies, or Urban Affairs, seems to be emerging as a new academic field, although some think that the subject presently lacks a sufficient body of substantial scholarship to qualify as an academic discipline. At an LRPC meeting with representatives of the disciplines currently offering courses related to Urban Studies, there was considerable disagreement over such questions as clarity of definition, development of theory, and self-sufficiency of method. A variety of organizational arrangements for including this area in the curriculum have been developed: formation of fieldwork centers and research institutes, formal interdisciplinary programs, provision for concentrations drawn largely from existing course offerings, or simply the addition to traditional disciplines of new courses dealing with the urban aspects of the field, for example, urban politics and mass transportation, urban renewal planning, the sociology of youth gangs. In addition, there is a discipline—geography—which seems to be absorbing in urban geography much of the subject matter generally regarded as Urban Studies. The possibility of a five-college approach to geography, with emphasis on urban geography as the cooperative specialty, is worthy of consideration, but the LRPC does not recommend the establishment of such a department now.

Urban Studies is obviously relevant and urgent in terms of contemporary social and academic concerns, and an impressive array of courses in this area currently exists among the five colleges. A recent proposal for graduate work in Urban Studies listed ten departments at the University offering eighty relevant courses taught by more than forty scholars. The other colleges probably provide as many more. Mount Holyoke offers an interdisciplinary major in Urban Studies. Smith offers a concentration in Urban Studies within a disciplinary major in economics, government, or sociology. There is little doubt that a five-college effort to coordinate and expand the offerings is needed and that it would be welcome. More than thirty faculty members from all institutions, for example, accepted invitations to attend a meeting in the spring of 1969 to discuss the establishment of the proposed five-college Field Office for Urban and Regional Studies (see Section V.B). There was enthusiastic endorsement for the creation of this facility, and with its appearance there will be increased opportunity to coordinate the strengthening of Urban Studies among the colleges.

The LRPC believes that Urban Studies can best be served by the creation of an interdisciplinary Council as described in Section II.A, above. The growth and maintenance needs of Urban Studies are essentially the same as those of area studies, and the presence of a field office will require a group of faculty and students through whom the director of the office can keep in touch with the academic programs of the institutions.

RECOMMENDATION

A five-college faculty-student Urban Studies Council should be established, with responsibility for investigating the possibilities for coordinated development of courses and programs.

4. THE ARTS

The Long Range Planning Committee believes that co-operative planning may be especially profitable in the arts because of:

- the unique skills of many individual artists;
- the wide range of talents required by many enterprises in the arts, especially when the visual arts, music, dance, and drama are joined, as in the theater or film;
- the growing interest of students in creative studies;
- the probable expansion of programs in the creative arts on some campuses where they have been relatively un-developed;
- the present state of building plans and discussions of space requirements for the arts on several campuses;
- the high cost of arts facilities, materials, and production.

The LRPC appointed three committees, one on the Performing Arts (music, dramatic art, dance), another on the Fine Arts (drawing, painting, sculpture, architecture), and a third on Film. Faculty and student representatives from the five colleges were appointed to each of the committees, and this section of the report draws heavily upon the documents they submitted.

a. Performing Arts

Examples of present cooperation in the performing arts are the Smith-Amherst Summer Theater, the Mount Holyoke-University and Smith-Amherst orchestras, the five-college electronic music studio at Hampshire, a joint calendar of Valley musical events, and exchange enrollments of Amherst students in applied music courses at Smith and the University. Harmony appears to have been achieved best by the musicians.

The Performing Arts Committee was somewhat dubious about the possibilities of doing more than is now being done to further cooperative activities. Though a marked growth of student interest in the arts was noted, and though the students on the committee strongly expressed their hope for increased participation in the programs of neighboring colleges, major impediments to cooperation were emphasized by the committee. Among these were insufficient faculty and a shortage of physical space, which sometimes prevent a college from accommodating more than a few students from other colleges. Overlapping schedules of production, perhaps inevitable in view of the limited time available, together with transportation problems, have prevented participation of more than a few students from neighboring campuses in the productions of another college. Differing curricular attitudes and course scheduling conflicts were other reasons given for relatively little student exchange in the performing arts. The lack of joint planning of new building facilities for the performing arts probably has resulted in less complementarity than could have been the case.

Nevertheless, several specific suggestions for achieving greater vitality and efficiency through cooperative planning grew out of the discussions of the advisory committee:

- the development of a five-college bulletin on the arts;
- a catalogue of teaching aids, such as slides, films, and books, and an inventory of costumes, lighting, and stage sets;
- the development of technical resources on a five-college basis—for example, the creation of a five-college costume shop;
- the joint support of resident artists, individuals or groups, for varying lengths of time, to give master classes and performances;
- the sharing of teaching specialists, as in playwriting, Oriental theater, ethnomusicology, and mixed media;
- a Five College Opera Company;
- a student art center where students of all the colleges could meet for exchange of ideas, exhibits, and to meet visiting artists;
- more joint or exchange exhibitions;

• creation of a summer arts festival.

The students on the Performing Arts Committee recommended that the five colleges sponsor a summer arts curriculum with an eye to performances and exhibits at the conclusion of eight weeks' work. The LRPC believes the proposal to be of sufficient interest to warrant some description.

Participants in the program would be students of the five colleges, selected from applicants to the appropriate department at the home institution. The teachers would be faculty members of the Art, Music, Dramatic Arts, and Dance Departments of the five colleges. Each department would direct its own program, concentrating on performance. Some degree of cooperation among departments could culminate in performances involving as many disciplines as possible, such as musical theater.

The present Smith-Amherst Summer Theater could serve as a model for the theater program. The music program could be centered on the performance of chamber, vocal, and keyboard music, which would lead to a variety of recitals presented at different times and locations. The fine arts program would give the student time in the studio and the chance to exhibit his work. The dance program would involve study in different areas of dance and choreography, with the goal again being performance. All the students might live in the dormitories of one of the five colleges. This would promote a constant exchange of ideas, and the personal contacts developed would increase the base for further five-college cooperation during the regular academic year. Sources of financial support of the program would include box office proceeds, foundation grants and/or alumni gifts and institutional subsidies.

b. Fine Arts

The Fine Arts Committee appointed by the LRPC reported that its early discussions revealed that the members lacked information about each other's departments. Accordingly, they arranged to exchange course lists and staff rosters. It turned out that the committee members in the past had been wasting much time and paper sending notices to individuals who were no longer teaching in the Valley and neglecting the new arrivals. They suggested that means be found to better inform students and advisers of courses at other institutions and that a Calendar of Art Events, published frequently, would assist interdepartmental communication.

The committee also noted that very little use is made of the faculties of other institutions. The only exchange taking place last year was between Mount Holyoke and the University. The committee suggested that faculty exchanges and other ways of enriching the teaching program be explored, particularly at the upper levels. Student exchange is also rather slight because of transportation and scheduling difficulties. More frequent exchange of students through better scheduling could lead to the very real possibility of introducing five-college programs in specific art areas (studio or art history). To coordinate exhibitions more precisely, it was suggested that a standing committee of the chairmen of each college's exhibition committee meet from time to time to consider both packaged exhibitions from outside the Valley and local exhibits of student and faculty work.

All the institutions, with the possible exception of Amherst College, lack sufficient studio space for undergraduates when they are not in formal classes. The Fine Arts Committee pointed to the educational advantage of bringing students together in a common area, for in the process of working in proximity there can be much useful discussion and criticism. The suggestion was made that a centrally located building, barn, or shed be found which could shelter this activity. It would be a common meeting and working area for those interested in the problems of art.

The need for a photographic facility is similar in part to

the need for a painter's barn, but with the added requirement that there be more special equipment available, such as darkrooms and photographic equipment. No single institution appears to have any such facility where students not enrolled in a formal class can try out artistic and inventive ideas in this medium. The advantages of centralizing this facility would be both financial and educational.

A proposal for a Center for Experimental Media prepared by a University committee with members from all five institutions was of considerable interest to the Fine Arts Committee. Whether the program outlined can be implemented depends upon the availability of funds and space.

Finally, the committee believed that there were ways in which the art library facilities could be better used and suggested that several art librarians meet to work out possibilities such as inter-library loan, Xerox copying, cooperative buying of expensive books and serials, and the preparation of a fine arts union catalogue.

c. Film

Student interest in the study and production of films is now making itself felt in the Valley and will, it seems likely, increase in the years ahead. The five colleges have responded with various plans for curricular offerings and provisions of space for film study and production.

Film entered the curriculum at the University four years ago when a course on the history of film was introduced by the Speech Department. A new course in theory and criticism was offered in the spring of 1969, and a course in "Radio-Television, Film, and Society" is given in both semesters. A basic film production course will begin in the fall of 1969, using 16 mm. equipment and with enrollment limited to between ten and fourteen students per section. The Speech Department does not regard its program as preprofessional, nor as a potential separate department. Emphasis will remain on the conceptual-historical-critical approaches to film;

a second one-semester course in film production will be perhaps the limit of offerings in that area.

Facilities for film at the University are now limited; the program uses what space it can find. A small studio, two screening rooms, and an editing suite are proposed for the projected Arts Center. The University is seeking to recruit someone to teach both film and television production. Most of the films shown in the history course are rented, though a very modest library of 8 mm. and 16 mm. films has been started by the Speech Department. Up to now there has been little integration of studies of film and video tape.

The future course of film studies at the University is not determined. A full-time consultant in mass communications has been in residence, and at the conclusion of the academic year 1968–69 he was to submit his full recommendations in film and related communications studies to the University.

Smith now has a course in still photography and will offer a mixed-media course this fall. Retrospective and foreign film series have been offered for many years. Next spring the Art Department will offer a one-semester course in film, historical and critical. Enrollment will be limited to twenty-five, with perhaps one-third of the students admitted from the other colleges.

Although there is provision for film study at Mount Holyoke, no courses in film are now being taught. The College has a regular series of film showings, and a second series is planned by a committee designing showings of coherent groups of films.

At Amherst, 165 students in eleven sections of the Problems of Inquiry course in the Humanities spent four to five weeks of the spring, 1969, semester making films with Super 8 equipment provided by the College. One professor taught film-making in a studio course in the Art Department, and several students are doing independent work in film. In the spring of 1970, a film history and criticism course will be offered by the Dramatic Arts Department; discussion is under way with Smith about making this a joint offering.

With grant support from the National Endowment for the Humanities, Hampshire is now planning a Film Studies program as an important component of its Humanities and Arts curriculum. The college will soon add a full-time faculty member to teach both film history and production and will have space for film viewing, shooting, and editing in both its library and its projected Humanities and Arts building.

Two recent developments are of special significance for the cooperative development of film studies in the Valley. The first is the Amherst Film Unit, a student group interested in both the study and making of films and in encouraging these in the five colleges. It was organized in 1968, and its membership of approximately forty includes not only Amherst students but Mount Holyoke and Smith students as well. The Unit has had the use of cameras purchased by Amherst for the Problems of Inquiry course in exchange for the maintenance of the equipment. The Unit's activities are extracurricular, though several of its members are highly skilled and have assisted in the teaching of the film unit of the Problems of Inquiry course.

The second recent development is the joint membership of the four colleges in the University Film Study Center. Their membership in this new Harvard-based Center, and the possible separate membership of the University as well, will provide a means for cooperative development of five-college resources in film. The University Film Study Center was incorporated in the summer of 1968 by representatives of eight New England colleges and universities for the purpose of establishing an archive-library to support education and research in the history and criticism of cinema and television. The initial aim of the Center is to acquire a collection of films and tapes—primarily features, shorts, and documentaries—illustrating the art of the motion picture. Supporting documentation in the form of stills, film clips, scripts, scenarios, memorabilia, and historical equipment will be acquired as funds and opportunities permit.

Because of their small size the four private colleges asked

if they could join the center as a cooperative unit. On the condition that they offer a coordinated program in film history and criticism, they were admitted to membership as the "Western Massachusetts Consortium" as of July 1, 1969.

The annual membership fee for institutions ($2,500) will be divided equally among the four cooperating members. It is hoped that the University of Massachusetts will also join as a separate institutional member.

RECOMMENDATIONS

1. **Two Arts Councils should be established, one for the Fine Arts (drawing, painting, sculpture, ceramics, architecture, and other visual and plastic arts), and another for Performing Arts (music, dance, and dramatic arts). They should have both student and faculty representatives from each institution. Among the subjects the two Councils should consider are increased exchange of information concerning courses, faculty, and programs; coordination of course scheduling; faculty exchange and complementary hiring; coordination of events and exhibitions, and publication of a common calendar; cooperation in the use of facilities, materials, and libraries; a five-college summer program in the arts; and the proposal for a five-college Center for Experimental Media.**
2. **A five-college Film Council should be established to coordinate the colleges' film library acquisitions and the use of films from the University Film Study Center. It should explore the wide range of possibilities for complementary development of film courses, materials, spaces, and faculty. The present college representatives on the Center Committee might appropriately be made members of the Council.**

B. Faculty Seminars & Colloquia

In recent years, several kinds of interinstitutional colloquia and faculty seminars have been developed. The colloquia usually involve fairly large numbers of faculty and sometimes students attending talks by specialists from outside the Valley, although some depend on local speakers. Faculty seminars are ordinarily limited to ten or fifteen participants who meet for dinner and for discussion of a paper presented by a member of the seminar or by an outside specialist. Subjects of the seminars have included "Methodology in the Social Sciences," "Religion and Political Development," "New Perspectives in Latin American Affairs," and a series of seminars on non-Western studies which for several years were funded by the Ford Foundation grant in Asian and African Studies. During the past two years seminars have also been held on comparative political parties, communism, Latin American studies, medieval studies, and philosophy.

Comparative Studies

Several of the Valley seminars and colloquia devoted to comparative studies were discussed in the immediately preceding subsections on Area Studies. One conspicuously successful faculty seminar—on comparative political parties—deserves more attention as an example of the possibilities of broadening intercultural comparative studies to include the functions of social and political institutions. This seminar, which began in 1967, was originally proposed and coordinated by a faculty member at Mount Holyoke. Its purpose has been to develop an analytical framework for the comparative study of political parties.

Approximately twenty faculty members, mostly political scientists, have participated at one time or another. For the most part the participants in the seminar on comparative political parties have drawn on the resources of political scientists in the Valley for the preparation of papers, although occasionally scholars from outside the five-college area have been invited to participate. Each seminar is preceded by a social hour and dinner. The participants believe this informal contact is important in developing a personal basis for furthering cooperation. It is hoped that the seminar will develop a series of comparative categories that will provide a basis for a five-college student seminar in comparative parties. Beyond this, it has been suggested that the group might wish to broaden its base to include the comparative functions of other political and social institutions such as bureaucracies, legislatures and legislative processes, judicial systems, and executive arrangements. This might lead to the development of a series of comparative seminars on the functions of various political and social institutions on a five-college basis for the enrichment of both undergraduate and graduate curricula.

Atlantic Studies

Among a number of possibilities for additional five-college cooperation in comparative studies, special attention might be given to Atlantic Studies. Many institutions and social and political ideas and processes that originated in Western Europe and North America are being adapted for use throughout the remainder of the world. The Atlantic region has been producing the vague outlines of a new international system in its halting efforts to formulate and develop supranational interests (and organizations to promote them) as partial replacements for conflicting national interests. The concentration of curriculum within each institution on discipline-oriented studies covering particular countries, or on intercountry comparisons, needs to be supplemented by the larger perspectives of interinstitutional, interdisciplinary concentration on the Atlantic area as a whole.

The resources for the development of Atlantic Studies are at hand in the form of faculty members specializing in the pertinent areas of the social sciences and humanities, a number of course offerings dealing with broad aspects of the Atlantic Community, the University-sponsored Atlantic Studies Program at Freiburg, and the Mount Holyoke program of summer internships in international and regional organizations. The task of examining the possibility that such relatively unrelated resources might be consolidated through five-college cooperation into the basis for a fresh approach to Western Studies remains open to the interest and initiative of appropriate members of the faculties of the Valley institutions.

Financial Support

The LRPC believes that faculty seminars and colloquia are an important part of the intellectual climate in the Valley and a vital means for faculty members to keep abreast of new developments in their fields. They may also prove to be the means for developing new levels of five-college cooperation in research, teaching methods, and curriculum revision.

The LRPC recognizes that five-college cooperation in colloquia and faculty seminars cannot be forced. But it does believe that it should be encouraged, especially in those areas of study in which faculty initiative is, or promises to be, effective in utilizing the resources of the five colleges for educational innovation. The possibilities of cooperation through the faculty seminars (and their eventual effect on research, teaching and curricular change) cover so many potential areas of study that we make no attempt to catalogue them. Although some of the attempts to develop faculty seminars will undoubtedly prove to be inadequate, the successful results of several of the existing seminars should encourage further experimentation.

RECOMMENDATIONS

1. Department heads and other administrators should actively encourage the formation or continuation of cooperative colloquia and faculty seminars.
2. Under policies established by the Academic Policy Advisory Council, financial support should be provided for up to ten faculty seminars at $300–$500 each per year.
3. The participants in faculty seminars should consider the desirability of organizing councils similar to the proposed Area Studies Councils for purposes of disseminating information and promoting both the appointment of complementary faculty specialists and the development of complementary library resources and courses of study.

C. Overseas Study Programs

THE OVERSEAS PROGRAMS of the five colleges vary greatly in type, scope, and underlying assumptions. They range from the University's summer Oxford Program, enrolling some 120 students, to Amherst's developing exchange program with Doshisha University. Little or no coordination among the programs exists.

Amherst College

Amherst has one overseas program, at Doshisha University, Kyoto, which was founded as Doshisha School in 1875 by an Amherst graduate. Amherst House, a residence building at Doshisha for twenty or thirty Japanese students particularly interested in American Studies, was established in

1932. Under the present relationship Amherst maintains a member of its faculty at Doshisha as a professor in residence and director of Amherst House. One or two Amherst College students go to Doshisha annually, after obtaining the B.A. degree at Amherst, to teach English, to assist in the Amherst House program, and to learn Japanese. Negotiations to widen the Amherst-Doshisha exchange are in progress.

A loosely structured exchange program between Amherst and the University of Warwick, England, will be in its third year in 1969–70, when two Amherst students will be there for the first semester. In addition, twenty to twenty-five Amherst students are expected to be abroad for academic year programs in 1969–70. Although information is made available to interested students, active encouragement to study abroad is not given, and it tends to be the more enterprising students who persevere and succeed in making the necessary arrangements. Many Amherst students go abroad in the summer, but usually not in formal study programs.

Mount Holyoke College

Mount Holyoke offers an unusual summer program of overseas study which is now in its twentieth year. Qualified juniors, seniors, or graduate students, who have had twelve hours in political science, including certain specified courses, are placed as volunteer assistants to work for two months for officials of the United Nations and its specialized agencies, regional organizations (for example, SEATO, NATO, OAS, OECD, Common Market), private international organizations such as the Carnegie Endowment, and foreign governments. Students from other colleges and universities may apply for admission to the program. In the past, participants have come from a number of other institutions, including Brandeis, Wheaton, Smith, and Stanford. Students pay their own travel and maintenance expenses, except the UNESCO interns, who receive stipends from UNESCO. A few Mount Holyoke students receive scholarships.

Mount Holyoke has a faculty exchange relationship with Women's Christian College at Madras, in India. In cooperation with other women's colleges in the United States, Mount Holyoke also participates in a thirteen-college faculty exchange program with women's colleges in India. In the last several years, this relationship has been relatively inactive.

Twenty-five Mount Holyoke students were enrolled in overseas institutions in 1968–69. Half were in the programs of other American colleges and universities, for example, Sweetbriar, Wayne State, Smith, and Hamilton, and half went independently to foreign universities. About a dozen Mount Holyoke students go abroad for summer study, some in the Oxford and Bologna programs of the University of Massachusetts. Many others go for travel only.

Smith College

Smith has operated junior year abroad programs since the 1920's. It now has programs in Geneva, Hamburg, Florence, Paris, Madrid, and Quezon City, the Philippines. The programs in Germany, Italy, France, and Spain are mainly for language majors. The Geneva program is primarily for students in economics, government, and sociology. The Philippines program, organized after discussions among the four colleges, is for students with special interests in Southeast Asia or developing countries. Under an agreement of 1945, Smith and the University of Toronto exchange four juniors annually. Special arrangements for study in sociology also exist with Leicester University.

Smith students enrolled in all its junior year abroad programs, except in the Philippines, retain their status as students of the college, and pay approximately the same amount for board, tuition, and residence as do students staying on campus. They finance their travel themselves. Students going to the Philippines take a leave of absence from Smith and are responsible for their own financial arrangements.

Also during the academic year Smith students who are

qualified majors in the Classics or Ancient Studies may spend one semester at the Intercollegiate Center for Classical Studies in Rome. Twenty-five American colleges and universities participate in this Center. Smith normally offers two summer abroad programs in art; these were held in Athens and Amsterdam in 1967 and in Paris and Vienna in 1969.

Because Smith offers such a variety of overseas study programs, it has not particularly encouraged students to study in the programs of other American colleges and universities unless these programs offer an unusual opportunity not available through the College's own programs. A few Smith students participate in the University's summer Oxford program (four in 1969); and for the first time two Smith students will be in the Bologna program this summer. No Smith students have been in the University's Madrid or Freiburg programs.

University of Massachusetts

The University operates for upper division and graduate students an academic-year program of study at the University of Freiburg, Germany. Although proficiency in German is a prerequisite, the program is not primarily for German majors, but offers advanced study in the humanities and social sciences. The program is open to students from other colleges and universities. The director of this program and an additional faculty member from the University of Massachusetts teach as visiting professors of the University of Freiburg.

Summer programs at Oxford, Bologna, and Madrid involve six weeks of course work, including supplementary lectures and excursions to major cultural centers, and about two weeks of independent travel. All are open to qualified students from other colleges and universities. The Oxford program, open to graduate and undergraduate students, offers courses in English literature taught by Oxford dons. Students have access to the Bodleian Library and live in Trinity College. The Madrid program of advanced studies in Spanish literature is designed mainly for graduate students, but accepts well qualified undergraduates who have taken the requisite three years of Spanish. Courses are taught by prominent Hispanists from Spain or Latin America and students live with Spanish families. In Bologna students take regularly scheduled University of Massachusetts courses at the Johns Hopkins Center on subjects in which the Italian location contributes significantly to the student's understanding and experience: art, history, language, government. The program is staffed primarily by University of Massachusetts faculty, although two Mount Holyoke professors have participated.

Preliminary planning has been undertaken to set up three new programs: a summer program in French language and literature in Pau, France; a summer program in intensive German in Freiburg, Germany; and a semester program in education at the New University of Ulster, Coleraine, Northern Ireland.

In 1874 the President of what is now the University of Massachusetts helped to establish the University of Hokkaido at Sapporo, Japan, and close ties have been maintained between the two institutions. Faculty members of each institution visit or teach or study at the other from time to time. The Universiy does not at present send students to Hokkaido, but the relationship between the two institutions may in the future facilitate a program of student exchange.

Hampshire College

Hampshire intends to offer its students as many opportunities for overseas experience as possible. The program of each student will be designed to fit his or her individual interests and needs. Some students may enroll in foreign universities independently; others may work abroad or enroll in foreign programs of American universities or combine travel with residence in foreign homes. One definite element in Hampshire's overseas programs at this stage of its planning is an agreement with the Mount Hermon School that Hampshire students may go abroad in Mount Hermon's summer abroad programs, some as regular student participants, others as program guides.

Possibilities for Five-College Cooperation

Five-college cooperation in the field of overseas study has so far been minimal and on an ad hoc basis. The five institutions operate quite different programs based on varying philosophies. Nevertheless, there are several ways in which cooperation would benefit all institutions.

There is no pooling of information among the five colleges on possibilities of low-cost travel for students wanting to go abroad. A combined effort in this area would save time, effort, and money for both the institutions and the students they advise. Although the summer five-college charter flights are cheaper than regular commercial flights, students can, through other charters, obtain cheaper international travel. Five-college charter flights have so far been utilized by only one summer study abroad program, the University's program in Bologna, but if the service could be expanded to offer more flexible and cheaper rates, it might be possible to use it for most student travel.

Cooperation in disseminating information to students on opportunities for overseas travel, work, and study is another area which has been neglected. As it requires an enormous amount of time to accumulate, keep up-to-date, and evaluate these various opportunities, pooling of information should be useful to all five institutions. Joint scheduling of the visits of recruiters for overseas study programs from outside the Valley, like the Experiment in International Living, might be part of this cooperative effort. The colleges could also share information on programs that are of poor quality or even fraudulent, and steer recruiters for these programs away from the Valley.

The University has employed Mount Holyoke faculty twice in its Bologna program, but beyond this there has been no cooperation in recruitment of directors or faculty for the various overseas programs. The prospects for more cooperation, in fact, are dim, because part of an institution's interest in having overseas programs lies in the opportunity for its own faculty to go abroad not at their own expense. Cooperation in recruitment of faculty and directors might therefore require some reciprocity among the five colleges. Five-college recruitment of faculty for study abroad programs would appear most feasible for new programs that might be initiated as five-college enterprises. Very preliminary investigation is being made of the possibility of a five-college junior year in England. If this or other five-college programs are established, it is conceivable that the directorship might rotate among participating institutions. Overall direction and continuity might then be provided through a five-college committee.

Cooperation in the recruitment of students for overseas programs has also been limited and requires better channels of information on existing programs among the Valley institutions. It is not expected that any college will encourage its students to enroll in the study abroad programs of the other institutions merely because they exist and need students to function, but each institution might at least make a more positive effort to see that its students learn about these programs. This requires that each institution designate the office to which information should be sent.

International Study Abroad in the Future

Many more five-college students will probably want to go abroad ten years hence than do today. Some kind of overseas experience might be expected for as much as twenty per cent of the student body annually. The cost of going abroad need not be a deterrent even now if students were better informed on ways of participating in international education cheaply. The trend towards more flexibility in degree requirements may eliminate a major deterrent to overseas study, the difficulty of meshing it with the student's degree program.

Most of the students going abroad will probably not go in structured programs, such as junior year abroad or for intensive academic study to earn credits, but will go to gain experience. Many students, especially from the private colleges, already go with this aim, and more would do so if they knew how.

The five colleges should have a continuing system for sharing information and resources for international education for all Valley students. They should utilize and share the experience and contacts of their staff (including visiting foreign professors) and students who have been abroad to create opportunities for students to live and study in foreign countries in programs tailored to individual needs. On his return home a foreign professor who was visiting lecturer in a Valley college might serve as adviser to a few students who return with him to study at his institution. Contacts made by Valley faculty abroad for research or sabbatical leave could be similarly utilized. One-, two-, or five-college programs of work-study abroad could be open to all Valley students. Students at colleges having a Four-One-Four academic calendar will have the opportunity for special one-month midwinter programs abroad: residence with a family in Quebec, a drama course in London, and a public health internship in the Caribbean are among the many possible programs.

It should be agreed that no one college will launch formal overseas study programs without consultation with the others. Cooperation may mean five-college direction or it may mean only initial five-college consultation. Many countries, especially in Europe, have already reached the saturation point in accepting new study programs from American institutions. Five-college cooperation in starting new programs should be initiated, both in the interests of the foreign countries and to enable new programs to draw on as wide a range of resources as possible. As additional formal overseas study programs of the Valley institutions are started, they should be distributed among the developed and developing nations.

RECOMMENDATION

A five-college committee should be appointed to explore the possibility of cooperation in overseas study activities and to prepare recommendations for instituting and sustaining such cooperation. It should establish a mechanism for exchanging information on these programs.

D. Joint Departments

SEVERAL KINDS of arrangements for coordinated academic planning are possible, as discussed in Section I.A of this report. Introductory work can be offered by departments on each campus, with advanced work coordinated to avoid duplication; most advanced work can be concentrated at one or two institutions; a strong department at one institution can offer most introductory and advanced work, with related courses available at the other institutions. Probably the ultimate means for coordinating course offerings in a particular field among the five institutions is the creation of a formal joint department with one chairman or head. Although the joint department structure has been suggested for other fields from time to time, most recently for History of Science, the only field for which it has been established is astronomy. Some history of the subject in the Valley may be a useful prelude to description of the joint department.

Astronomy in the Valley

Astronomy was introduced into the Amherst curriculum in the 1830's, and an observatory building was erected in 1853. With the installation in that year of an equatorial telescope, the Amherst College Observatory became one of the major observatories in the country. Observatories at Mount Holyoke and Smith were founded in 1881 and 1885, respectively, and a new observatory was constructed at Amherst in 1905. During the first half of the twentieth century, however, the relative importance of astronomy in the Valley diminished because the individual colleges could not keep pace with developments at larger observatories throughout the country.

The Joint Astronomy Department

The conditions for reversing this decline came with the creation of the Four College Astronomy Department which resulted from negotiations among astronomers at the Valley institutions between 1958 and 1960. The plan of development as it was then put forth focused on undergraduate teaching. The astronomers, who had experienced great difficulties in recruiting personnel and in improving equipment, hoped that in collaboration they might find a means of solving their problem. They hoped first to increase flexibility and mobility. A, for example, might teach B's courses, should B wish to visit an observatory located at some distance during the appropriate time of the year; B, in turn, could reciprocate for A. The astronomers were concerned, too, with library resources and hoped to maintain and strengthen an excellent existing collection housed at Amherst. Their report mentions a number of additional advantages: a four-college department would be a good public relations move; foundations would consider more carefully proposals issuing from a joint department; sharing the cost would permit the purchase of better equipment; and a wider variety of courses would grace the several catalogues. All, in short, would benefit from closer intellectual and disciplinary contacts.

Four-college (now five-college) astronomy has developed in a fashion that meets and in some respects even exceeds the expectations of the founders. Enrollments have increased. In 1965–66, 747 students were enrolled in the several introductory courses; in 1968–69 there were 1,381. On the advanced four-college level, only 18 students were enrolled during 1965–66; in the current year, 110. The University, a junior partner in 1960, has now assumed leadership. The faculty has grown from five plus one Post-Doctoral Fellow in 1965–66 to ten plus six Post-Doctoral Fellows in 1968–69. Federal research support has grown in the last three years from $17,000 to about $400,000 annually.

The department, which now offers a Ph.D. program, includes among its faculty members a leader in the field of infrared astronomy, the discoverer of variability in quasars, the first American to discover a pulsar, an expert on galaxy formation, and another on the nature of the clouds of Venus. With its younger colleagues, one each at Amherst, Mount Holyoke, and Smith, this is clearly a department of distinction, and its chairman certainly has reason to hope that it may equal the leaders at the California Institute of Technology, Princeton, and Berkeley. The library resources are excellent.

Future Plans

Plans include projects in both teaching and research. The department hopes to offer, at the University, majors both for those who intend to go on to graduate work in astronomy and for those whose purpose is limited to secondary school teaching or scientific journalism. It will continue its graduate program both for the Ph.D. and for the terminal M.A. Various techniques to overcome transportation and scheduling problems, among them closed circuit television and taped lectures, are being explored.

The research of the future will depart substantially from classical optical observation. New England weather seriously limits optical observation, and the five-college department proposes major programs in that field only in collaboration with other institutions which might construct a telescope in the Southwest or in South America. The major observational thrust in the department will be in radio astronomy, which is less costly to support and which has the added advantage of feasibility in a cloudy, overcast region. Infrared astronomy will also receive support, and the theoretical sector will continue its development.

Problems

Despite these advances, there are certain problems. The University has seven teaching astronomers plus researchers, while Amherst, Mount Holyoke, and Smith each have one astronomer. It has not always been easy to relate the programs and projects at the research-oriented University with the needs and expectations of colleges dedicated to undergraduate instruction. The situation is complicated by the fact that a college, in deciding matters of tenure and promotion, must take cognizance of recommendations from a university department chairman whose expectations may differ from those of the undergraduate institution. These stresses appear to be no greater than those of any department comprising both graduate and undergraduate teaching, but the lack of a five-college "court of appeals," so to speak, sometimes prevents their resolution.

There is also need for more equipment, especially for a radio astronomy facility for both graduate and undergraduate research. Technicians are needed to service the infrared group, and another desideratum is expanded facilities in laboratory astrophysics. A larger telescope for undergraduate teaching is badly needed, and such an addition would facilitate certain types of research as well.

Other Possible Joint Departments

Occasional courses in the History of Science have been taught in one or another of the Valley colleges for many years. In 1957 it was suggested that the subject might be handled cooperatively, but not until 1960 was a joint appointment made with costs divided by the private colleges. In a subsequent appointment, the University also shared in the costs. In 1967 a five-college committee to consider the future of History of Science recommended that more faculty be appointed and that they be organized into a joint department along the lines of the Astronomy Department. The Presidents, although they agreed that several faculty members might be sought, made no commitment on the organization of a new formal joint department. They did not, however, rule out the idea. History of Science is discussed further in the following section.

RECOMMENDATIONS

1. **The Academic Policy Advisory Council should discuss the Five College Astronomy Department and assist in resolving any conflict there may be between its undergraduate and graduate interests.**
2. **The Academic Policy Advisory Council should consider whether, and under what conditions, the joint department provides a suitable structure for coordinating course offerings in other fields of study.**

E. Joint Appointments

FROM TIME TO TIME two or more colleges have made joint appointments of faculty either to supplement the work of some department or to provide courses not sufficiently in demand to justify the appointment of a full-time teacher by one institution. An early example—an appointment in the Departments of Economics at both Smith and Amherst—is recorded in the 1956 *Report of the Committee on Cooperation.* A one-semester joint appointment, supported by the Ford Foundation grant for Asian and African Studies, was made in 1965–66 by the Department of Political Science at Mount Holyoke and the Department of Government at the University of a professor to teach courses on contemporary Chinese politics.

History of Science

The most notable recent examples of the joint appointment have been two successive appointments in History of Science. The cost of the first was borne by the three private colleges. The second was supported by all four institutions.

Interest in the History of Science has a respectable local history. Pioneer scholars, notably at Amherst, Mount Holyoke, and the University, had long taught in the field before four-college cooperation suggested opportunities for development during the late 1950's. Four-college committees were organized which recommended the two successive appointments mentioned above. To each of these historians of science, Smith initially or eventually offered affiliation to assure salary payment, provide fringe benefits, and regularize departmental status. Experience demonstrated that while recruiting might be conducted on a collaborative basis and costs might be shared, responsibility for administration should lie with one institution. Both appointees offered courses on more than one campus to students from all four institutions.

At an early period in the program, the four-college committee considered the concurrent appointment of a second historian of science. Encouraged by the evidence of growing student demand, increasingly aware of the practical difficulties confronted by a single appointee making his way among several institutions, the committee in 1967 recommended the creation of a joint department patterned after the Four College Astronomy Department. The committee hoped that such a department might contain specialists in the several areas of ancient, medieval, and early modern science as well as in the modern history of biological and physical science. The department might best fulfill an additional function as a bridge between the sciences and the humanities by continuing and developing courses in such areas as science and public policy and the philosophy of science. Although the Presidents agreed that several historians of science were needed in the Valley, they did not commit themselves to a formal joint department. The present History of Science Committee, therefore, is assisting the several institutions willing to bring a historian of science onto their faculties, and attempting to coordinate such appointments so that specialties will be complementary.

Five College Scholars

Joint appointments of individual faculty members for a long term present problems. The lack of an institutional "home" is unsettling, evaluation of performance uncertain, and channels for promotion and the granting of tenure are unclear. Hence, as has been noted above, the practice of making one institution administratively responsible has been adopted.

It may be that the joint appointment device would prove more useful for temporary appointments of visiting lecturers of benefit to two or more of the institutions. A more ambitious suggestion is that all five institutions join in an annual appointment of a particularly distinguished scholar.

The field to be represented might change each year. Five-college faculty committees could be appointed on an ad hoc basis to suggest nominees for the scholar well in advance and to propose a program for him. In time, if it were carefully developed, the Five College Visiting Scholar program could achieve great distinction.

RECOMMENDATIONS

1. **The Academic Policy Advisory Council should consider the circumstances in which joint appointments are useful and should establish guidelines for administering such appointments. It should also consider instituting a program of Five College Visiting Scholars.**
2. **The present History of Science Committee should continue its coordination of recruitment of faculty in that field.**

F. Graduate Programs

THE PROBLEM of academic complementarity and cooperation in graduate programs among the five colleges is one which is affected by the uneven balance between the four colleges, taken as a unit, and the largely self-sufficient University. The problem is exacerbated by the fact that although Smith, Mount Holyoke, and Amherst provide for limited graduate studies individually, the dominant commitment is to high-quality undergraduate programs in the liberal arts and sciences, while the University is increasingly concerned with development of graduate programs as an important, although by no means exclusive, part of its commitment to higher education.

The four colleges have all been involved in graduate programs of various types for a long period of time. However, only in the last decade has the University been actively engaged in expanding its graduate program in virtually all areas of its curriculum. Previously the University tended to concentrate its graduate work in those areas which were characteristic of its earlier role as Massachusetts Agricultural College. In the academic year 1968–69, the total graduate school enrollment at the University exceeded three thousand, or almost twenty per cent of the total student enrollment at the University's Amherst campus. The most recent projections anticipate an increase in graduate enrollments for the next decade to approximately ten thousand, which would represent about one-third of the projected University total student enrollment of thirty thousand. At the present time the doctorate is offered in more than forty areas of study within the University, including most of the fields in the liberal arts and sciences which have counterpart undergraduate programs in the other four colleges in the Valley. In approximately fifteen other fields, graduate work leading to the master's degree is offered. The University has tripled in enrollment during the past decade, but the graduate program has grown proportionately at a much greater pace. Not only has the graduate program expanded into practically all fields previously covered by the undergraduate instructional program at the University, but in recent years new graduate programs have developed in areas in which the University has not previously offered a full-scale undergraduate curriculum, for example, labor relations.

Among the other colleges, Smith has the most extensive program of studies leading to higher degrees, much of it in specialized areas. In 1968, Smith awarded 122 graduate degrees. The largest number was in the School for Social Work, with others in Education, Fine Arts, Physical Education, and a variety of subjects in the liberal arts. Although no Ph.D. degrees were awarded in 1968 or 1969 other than those in the cooperative degree program, three Ph.D.'s have been awarded at Smith in recent years.

Mount Holyoke currently enrolls about fifty graduate students working toward M.A.'s in various fields of the liberal arts and for the Master of Arts in Teaching. Normally, Mount Holyoke awards about fifteen master's degrees each year. Amherst awards an M.A. on occasion, and at one time a fairly steady flow of M.A. students was enrolled, especially in the languages. At present Amherst has no M.A. enrollments.

The most important expression of four-college cooperation at the graduate level is the cooperative Ph.D. program. This program, which was approved by the University of Massachusetts Graduate Council and by the faculties of Amherst, Mount Holyoke, and Smith in 1959, provides that the cooperative Ph.D. degree be awarded by the University but that the student's residence and most of his work (in some cases all of it) may be in any one of the four institutions. Degrees awarded under this program carry a notation on the diploma, the permanent record card, and all transcripts to the effect that it is a cooperative Ph.D. degree involving Amherst, Mount Holyoke, and Smith Colleges and the University of Massachusetts. The requirements are identical with those for the Ph.D. at the University, except that for the cooperative degree residence is defined as the institution in which the thesis work is done. The Graduate Council of the University, subject to the approval of the University's Board of Trustees, determines general policy, approves the course and degree requirements, sets the admissions policies, and appoints the thesis committees. The Graduate Council contains, in addition to a representative membership from the University, a member from each of the participating colleges, selected in accordance with established procedures for making such appointments by the various institutions.

Participation by departments in the cooperative Ph.D. program is on a voluntary basis. Following the approval of the cooperative arrangement, the biological sciences was the first group of departments to organize a cooperative Ph.D.

program, in the fall of 1959, and their action was followed shortly thereafter by the development of programs in languages (German, French, and Spanish) and in chemistry, physics, geology, and philosophy. In addition to these eight fields, the Four College Department of Astronomy offers graduate work at the Ph.D. level as part of the graduate work in the physics and astronomy program based at the University.

The first Four College Ph.D. was awarded in 1961, and through June, 1969, seventeen additional cooperative Ph.D.'s were conferred. In the academic year 1968–69, some 125 students are listed as officially registered in this program. This figure, however, is grossly misleading. The number is inflated because four departments or departmental divisions at the University—French, German, Spanish, and philosophy—continue to offer the Ph.D. only under the cooperative rubric, although in point of fact most of the graduate students in these areas are enrolled in the University and are doing all of their work there. The figures in the biological sciences and chemistry, in both of which the University continues to participate in the cooperative Ph.D. program while offering a complete Ph.D. program within the University departments, reflect much more realistically the extent of the cooperative program. The current enrollments for the cooperative Ph.D. in these areas are four and five students, respectively. This means that the number of graduate students who are effectively enrolled in the program is about twenty-five to thirty, a figure which is much more congruent with the previously cited actual number of degrees awarded. Until the departments at the University which are officially credited with large numbers of four-college students take the steps to secure approval of independent Ph.D. programs, the actual numbers involved will continue to be skewed in this fashion.

The state of the cooperative Ph.D. program is a good starting point for appraising the change that has occurred in the relationship of the University to the other colleges in graduate studies. When the cooperative Ph.D. program was established, the University did not have an adequate library or sufficient faculty resources, either in numbers or prestige, to initiate effective graduate programs in certain fields. The cooperation of the colleges was essential to the University's development as a graduate institution. The situation today is quite different. In all of the areas in which the cooperative Ph.D. is offered the University now has a sufficiently diversified faculty to carry out its graduate program independently. The University library has been greatly enlarged and is growing rapidly, although in some fields the collections at the colleges continue to be important for graduate study. In a sense, one might say that the University originally had much more to gain from cooperation at this level than the other colleges, whereas today the University is in the position of being able to provide an opportunity for the colleges to participate in a fully developed graduate program to the extent that they may desire to do so. The implications of this change are discussed further below.

Apart from the cooperative Ph.D. program, cooperation at the graduate level has been much more informal and therefore much more difficult to appraise in specific terms. The original plan for the four-college Ph.D. program provided that qualified faculty members at any of the four colleges could be elected to membership on the graduate faculty of the University, regardless of whether the departments of such faculty members at the other colleges were involved in the program. On the latest count, the graduate faculty of the University consists of approximately 975 members. Of these, more than 90 are faculty members of the other colleges. A perusal of the list discloses that while most of these faculty members are drawn from the departments participating in the cooperative Ph.D. program, a substantial number are from areas not formally included in it. This distribution suggests, and a casual sample of views confirms, that there is considerable reciprocal interest in four-college graduate cooperation at the faculty level on an individual basis.

To the extent that University departments still lack specialists in certain subfields or require replacements on a temporary basis, they turn to the other colleges in the Valley to supplement their graduate offerings. Faculty members from the other colleges also participate occasionally in graduate seminars or colloquia at the University and sometimes serve as members of examining committees for University candidates for higher degrees. In turn, departments at the University are frequently called upon by the colleges to recommend graduate students to serve as examination readers for large lecture courses or as research assistants. Some graduate students also take courses for graduate credit at the other colleges under the usual rules for student exchange. Although not easily measured because of lack of consistent reporting, informal arrangements at the graduate level add up to a considerable amount of cooperative exchange.

Perhaps the most critical question regarding the possibilities of future cooperation at the graduate level is the extent to which Amherst, Hampshire, Mount Holyoke, and Smith may wish to maintain an association with a fully developed graduate program in order to satisfy certain perceived needs of their respective faculties in both teaching and research. This issue is by no means settled. Some faculty members and administrators hold firmly to the view that the attraction of undergraduate instruction at liberal arts colleges of the caliber of those in the Valley is sufficient to enable them to recruit and retain superior faculty members. Others argue that, with the increasing specialization of fields and subfields and the research orientation characteristic of most departments in the major graduate schools, younger faculty members will increasingly prefer to go to large institutions with widely diversified faculties, opportunities to teach graduate students, and enhanced possibilities for research. Certainly few would contend that a mediocre graduate program is inherently more attractive than a liberal arts college with students of the highest quality. At the same time, there are discernible differences between the teaching and supervision of research of first-rate graduate students and the teaching of even the best undergraduate students, the most notable being in the relative degree of professional commitment on the part of the student.

Considerable evidence could be adduced to demonstrate that many departments of the University are increasingly competitive on a national basis when measured against such criteria as the ability to attract graduate faculty in both the senior and junior ranks, the capacity to recruit first-rate graduate students from a wide spectrum of institutions, the quality of institutions at which students with University Ph.D.'s are placed, and its enhanced reputation as a place in which research scholars thrive. Furthermore, the University has now grown sufficiently to be able to provide equipment, particularly in the natural sciences, that is sometimes beyond the reach of even the best financed private liberal arts colleges.

Faculty needs in the graduate area vary considerably from discipline to discipline. People in the sciences generally require more association with fellow specialists and graduate students and more elaborate equipment than do those in the social sciences and the humanities. But even in the latter areas, cooperative research and access to computers, research assistants, and colleagues in the same or closely allied fields are becoming more important.

The opportunity for faculty members at the colleges to participate in the University's graduate program could be extended, on an individual voluntary basis, beyond the limits of the present four-college cooperative Ph.D. program without excessive costs to the participating colleges. One suggestion is that the colleges provide a limited number of teaching or research assistantships for University graduate students. A mutually beneficial exchange could be developed in which a college faculty member teaches a graduate seminar at the University in return for some paid teaching or research assistantships for University graduate students at his college. The colleges already have some assistantships in their own graduate programs; those suggested here would be additional. If each of the four undergraduate colleges could establish, say, ten assistantships to be filled by graduate students from the University on the basis of demonstrated departmental need and desire for participation by individual faculty members, a natural basis for graduate cooperation would be built up. It seems likely that a graduate student serving as a reader or research assistant for one or more professors in one of the colleges would be inclined to work with one of them in the preparation of his graduate research project. The availability of the services of graduate assistants is a means of compensating faculty members for the time they may devote to graduate studies, without involving a reduction in undergraduate teaching loads.

Faculty seminars which have already been developed, and which form a potential basis for certain area study Councils, might also consider the possibility of extending their co-operative arrangements to the presentation of some five-college seminars at the graduate as well as the undergraduate level. Again, the value of such discussions would be to bring interested faculty members at the college into contact with the graduate program at the University, and in turn the University could benefit by the expanded participation of complementary faculty members at the other institutions.

Another area in which some explorations might be made is in the preparation of teachers for the state's junior colleges. The Graduate Council of the University addressed itself to this question last fall and came to the conclusion that community colleges had perhaps not been sufficiently encouraged to call on the University for the use of qualified graduate students in their instructional programs. At the present time Mount Holyoke, Smith, and the University all offer a Master of Arts in Teaching. Amherst students who wish to secure certification as teachers in the public school system usually go to Smith for their work in education and some of them go on to the M.A.T. degree there. In the light of anticipated needs in this area, interested departments should be encouraged to try to develop more intercollege cooperation in working with the community colleges to develop a program of graduate preparation for teaching at these institutions and to coordinate the two-year programs of the latter with the upper division offerings of the University and the colleges. The urgent needs of higher education, particularly in the public sphere, represent a challenge to both public and private institutions in the graduate area that might be better met through the combined experience of high-quality undergraduate institutions in cooperation with a university offering extensive graduate programs.

RECOMMENDATION

The Academic Policy Advisory Council should consider increased cooperation in graduate programs with a view to devising a more systematic method for bringing faculty members at the private colleges into direct contact with the University's graduate program, either by direct participation in the program or by finding opportunities to employ University graduate students in the educational activities of the colleges. It should recommend ways of attaining maximum advantage from the cooperative Ph.D. program and should explore the possibilities for improved cooperation in M.A.T. programs designed for potential community college teachers as well as for secondary school teachers.

III

Student Course Exchange

AT THE CENTER of the five-college enterprise is the opportunity for students to take courses at any of the five institutions. The whole apparatus for five-college cooperation exists for the primary purpose of bringing together those teachers and students who share a mutual interest in some particular field of study. All the admissions officers testify that the opportunity to take exchange courses plays an important part in attracting able students to the Valley colleges and to the University. In recent years, the number of students taking advantage of this opportunity has increased dramatically. Yet several problems still frustrate students attempting to gain the advantages of course exchanges. Other problems can be foreseen as emerging with the continued evolution of these exchanges. The precise statement of those goals which should govern the policies for course exchange remains a difficult problem in balancing educational objectives.

A. Goals

THE CLEAREST goal of course exchange is to make available to any student a specialized course within his major educational field of interest which is not available to him on his home campus. Thus, a history major at Amherst with an interest in Latin American history, a subject not regularly offered at Amherst, may take courses in this field at

Smith or the University. This was the original, basic rationale for course exchange, and it will certainly continue to be the heart of the program.

A second less clear but generally accepted goal for course exchange has emerged from four-college experience. This is to enable the student who, in choosing elective courses outside his major, wishes to explore a subject which is not available to him on his home campus, to do so. Thus, until sociology courses were begun at Amherst last year, an Amherst student wishing some experience with sociology could take a course at a neighboring institution. This opportunity for exploration is both possible and fairly prevalent under the existing arrangements, but it does raise questions. Will the course in question really foster the educational development of the student more than some other elective on the home campus? Does the student really know what he is undertaking and why? Are there legitimate educational reasons why his home institution does not offer such a course? May not a liberal arts institution quite properly hesitate to grant credit for a course in a professional school of the University just as the professional school at the University might hesitate to grant credit toward its degree for courses in the liberal arts at neighboring colleges? In these instances, in order that the opportunity for course exchange be used wisely, both the student and his advisers must know as much as possible about the course in question and about the student's reasons for taking it.

The LRPC believes that a third academic goal for course exchange is the opportunity to take a course at a neighboring institution which may overlap to some degree a course at the home institution but in which the educational experience promises to be significantly different from that of the home course. The catalogue title of the course may be the same, but there may be differences in the teacher's approach to the subject, the material covered, the work expected of students, or the course procedure—for example, a seminar instead of a lecture course.

Under the present formula for course exchange, when rigidly applied, there seems to be no opportunity for a student to take such an exchange course. Yet clearly in some cases this would be a valuable educational opportunity. It could well sharpen the insight and broaden the perspective with which a student returned to his home department and thus benefit his home institution as well as himself. The dangers, of course, would be that the "significantly different" features of the exchange course might be educational losses or unnecessary disruptions of a coherent program within the home department. Again, in making this kind of opportunity for course exchange available, the student and his advisers must know as much as possible about the course and about the student's reasons for taking it.

Finally, many students see as a goal of exchange courses the possibility of escaping from the "parochialism" of the home campus to gain valuable comparisons with their regular educational context by some study at another institution. Their reasons in this case are not strictly academic. One reason is unquestionably the aspiration of students to be more the masters of their own education. Obviously, the students at those institutions which are now segregated by sex feel most strongly the desirability of this goal for course exchange, though University students also testify to their desire for experiencing the educational atmosphere at the private colleges. Often students argue that it was this possibility as much as the more direct academic advantages of four-college exchange which attracted them to the Valley and express their disappointment at the difficulty they encounter in enrolling for exchange courses. The Five College Student Coordinating Board has proposed, in order to meet this goal, that every student should be permitted to take at least one exchange course in four years without regard to any academic criteria.

The members of the LRPC understand this natural student aspiration and see some merit in it. A student's experience with the academic life of another institution can enhance his perception of the characteristics of his home campus. We consider this experience to be a legitimate part of the goals in exchange courses. We do not, however, think that this goal should ever be allowed to override or to replace an academic justification for an exchange course. Any student who wishes the experience of taking a course on another campus can select such a course on the basis of one of the three academic criteria already described.

B. Growth of Exchange

Some of the significant present dimensions in course exchanges can be seen by reviewing the statistics for the past three years:

Year	*Total Undergraduate Semester Exchange Enrollment*
1966–67	581
1967–68	646
1968–69	1081

Further understanding of the nature of these exchanges can be gained by an institutional breakdown of these figures as shown in Table I.

It is clear from these statistics that the number of course exchanges has increased very significantly in the past year. We assume that exchanges will probably continue to increase. Certainly the addition of Hampshire College will provide a considerable net increase in the figures as its student population grows and moves into more advanced courses.

Considered in relation to the total of roughly 180,000

TABLE I

Semester courses taken by students from each of the four colleges at the others

Home Institution	66–7	67–8	68–9	66–7	67–8	68–9	66–7	67–8	68–9	66–7	67–8	68–9
	MOUNT HOLYOKE			SMITH			UNIVERSITY			TOTALS		
AMHERST	28	33	111	161	183	293	52	71	118	241	287	522
	AMHERST			SMITH			UNIVERSITY			TOTALS		
MOUNT HOLYOKE	24	30	85	29	28	43	62	38	65	115	96	193
	AMHERST			MOUNT HOLYOKE			UNIVERSITY			TOTALS		
SMITH	54	127	177	3	6	17	108	57	97	165	190	291
	AMHERST			MOUNT HOLYOKE			SMITH			TOTALS		
UNIVERSITY	28	25	36	7	12	5	25	36	34	60	73	75
							Grand Totals			581	646	1081

course registrations per year (from a Valley population of 22,300 students), the number of exchange courses taken during 1968–69 is small indeed. This may indicate that the present problem is perhaps more how to facilitate exchange courses than how to limit them. From this viewpoint, it would seem logical to conclude that some students who could reasonably benefit from exchange courses are somehow deterred from participating, rather than that too many students are taking exchange courses too haphazardly.

It may be, however, that much easier access to exchange courses would swamp the institutions. This calls for some forethought about reasonable ways to limit future exchanges if the present barriers of attitude, transportation, calendar, and schedule should be lowered.

The figures for separate institutions suggest both that internal institutional attitudes or policies have considerable impact on student exchange and that the present formula for exchange courses may unfairly limit the opportunity of students at the larger institutions. Amherst, which offers the fewest courses of its own, exports the highest proportion and even the highest number of students. The figures for University students taking courses at the other campuses may be low partly because until 1968–69 the University permitted its students to take exchange courses only if they were advanced students with a high academic average, and only in their major field. The figure may go up with the change in the announcement about exchange courses in the new catalogue and with increased publicity about exchange courses. It may also go up as the University initiates its new Honors Program, in which students are expected to make greater use of opportunities for exchange. Nonetheless, students at the University, which offers almost all courses found at any of the colleges, may be unreasonably handicapped by a formula which allows student eligibility only for a course "not available to him on his own campus" without recognizing differences in the nature of courses on a somewhat similar topic.

C. Present Difficulties

NOT ONLY the statistics but also the testimony of students indicate that there are presently barriers to course exchange which may limit unduly the legitimate educational advantages of the program:

Transportation: The difficulties of transportation and the consequent student time involved in any exchange course were eased somewhat by the new bus schedule last year. The problems of five-college transportation are discussed elsewhere in this report. Here we would simply note that geography has provided a built-in impediment to course exchange which will probably continue to restrain all except those students who see real personal benefits to be gained from an exchange course.

Schedule: The difficulties of fitting an exchange course into a student's course schedule are great. These may be eased somewhat, and have been already, as education continues to move toward seminars and more independent study and away from the pattern of frequent lectures and course meetings. The problem will then come to be how to fit exchange students into the smaller seminars and tutorial groups. Here some form of quota system may have to be devised on a reciprocal basis.

After consideration of the problem posed by Smith's unique weekly schedule, the LRPC has concluded that it is really difficult to know whether this three-consecutive-day pattern actually does make it more difficult for students to take exchange courses which require fitting Smith's schedule to the more normal pattern of every-other-day meetings. The evidence shows that each year the total of Smith students taking exchange courses and other students taking courses at Smith is almost as great as for any other institution. We are inclined to let this traditional talking-point among the five colleges rest until further evidence of its difficulty may come in.

Calendar: The full possibilities of course exchange are

handicapped by the differences in the academic calendars of the institutions. Although this problem has been lessened by consultation in recent years, semesters still begin at different times, and vacations and final examinations are not fully synchronized. Those students who have taken exchange courses agree that the different semester openings and the different vacations raise real inconveniences for students in exchange courses and deter others from taking such courses. It would seem possible to move toward calendars which begin and end the academic year simultaneously without significantly disturbing the educational autonomy of the separate faculties.

The difference in the scheduling of final examination periods is the one problem which raises educational difficulty as well as personal inconvenience for exchange students, and they think it should receive priority. This problem may be eased somewhat if the institutions move toward the more flexible examination schedule which is being tried at Amherst and Mount Holyoke.

There are a variety of programs which might facilitate course exchange. The adoption by all of the institutions of the Four-One-Four academic calendar, in which each institution might mount special academic programs in the January session, is recommended by the LRPC in Section IV. Another proposal which has been mentioned is the institution of special interdisciplinary programs, such as Science and Society, Communications, Environmental Studies, or Studies in War and Peace. If these were adopted on a five-college basis, and if they constituted the full program of students for a semester or a year, schedules and transportation could be coordinated so that exchange would be vastly simplified; for example, everyone in the program could have all courses at Amherst on Monday, at the University on Tuesday, and at Mount Holyoke on Wednesday.

Use of Libraries: The present policies and rules for the use of the library at one institution by a student from another, although they have not been arbitrarily established, are often frustrating to students. Only students actually enrolled in an exchange course are allowed to use the other institution's library, and their use of that library is generally restricted to meeting the requirements of the course. Students not enrolled in exchange courses must go through the regular inter-library loan procedures at their own institution to obtain a book, and this is sometimes subtly discouraged. Faculty members, even though they generally get preferential treatment in these matters, will understand the students' impatience at being so near and yet so far. On the other hand, the efficient operation of a library is never easy, even when the library is properly designed to give the right level of service to a population of a given size. Past experience with student use of home-campus libraries, and even more their use of other libraries, suggests that drastic liberalization of the present rules is simply an invitation to disaster. However, since it is predictable that an increase in exchange courses will aggravate the problems, some means should be sought to soften the present inflexibilities and to achieve a greater measure of understanding between borrower and lender. This problem is discussed in Section VIII.E of this report.

Approval for Course Exchange: The previous four difficulties limiting course exchange have a certain objectivity and intractability which most students can understand. The difficulties which impress students as arbitrary, artificial, and unnecessary have sometimes arisen in the process of seeking approval for exchange courses. Yet it is this process which faculty members consider to be at the heart of institutional integrity and educational responsibility. At its worst, the process leads students to see the faculty as defensive of personal interests rather than of principle and leads faculty members to see students as escaping from educational development rather than seeking it. The problem of advising students wisely on their educational program is difficult enough within any educational institution. It becomes immensely more complicated when it involves courses at another institution about which the adviser may know little and when it also involves student motives for educational experience which go beyond the strictly academic. There is a real need for making the procedures for approval of exchange courses as honest, informed, and rational as possible. For that reason, the LRPC proposes some modifications of the existing statement on course exchanges and of the process for reviewing student applications.

The present catalogue statement on exchange courses specifies that

> a student in good standing at any of the four institutions may take a course, without cost to the student,[1] at any of the other three if the course is not available to him on his own campus and he has the necessary qualifications. The course must have a bearing on the educational plan arranged by the student and his adviser. Approvals of the student's adviser and the Academic Dean of the College (Provost at the University) at the home institution are required.

This statement, when rigidly applied, recognizes only the first two goals for course exchange which we have described in Section A above. It does not allow for consideration of any course which may in its subject matter somewhat overlap one at the home institution but which still offers a significantly different educational experience, although there may be some variations in interpretation of its intent. Moreover, this statement does not recognize in any way what may be legitimate in a student's desire to take some academically reasonable course within the different context of another educational institution. Hence we propose revising this basic statement by striking out the words, "if the course is not available to him on his own campus," and substituting

[1] This phrase, it should be noted, does not relieve the student of paying the course *fees* (for individual musical instruction, laboratory or studio materials, etc.) at the receiving institution.

for them the following phrase: "if the course is significantly different from any available to him on his own campus."[2] In any discussion with an adviser this statement would slightly shift the emphasis toward consideration of the particular nature of the course and toward what the student hoped to gain educationally through these significant differences.

Greater efforts need to be made to ensure that relevant information is available both to students and advisers about courses at other institutions. (The Five College Student Coordinating Board has expressed interest in and willingness to work for the establishment of a clearinghouse for this purpose.) A systematic attempt to collect the syllabi or reading lists for courses would go a long way toward reducing the ignorance and arbitrariness which now necessarily accompany many of these decisions. Where publications like the Amherst course critique exist, they too might be used with the discretion appropriate for such publications.

In cases where the student and his adviser may be unable to reach agreement on a proposed exchange course, we recommend that each institution provide some process through which both student and adviser can gain further information about the nature of the proposed course and its suitability for the educational goals and program of the student and of the degree-granting institution. Where even this fails, the student should be allowed to take his case elsewhere, perhaps to his Dean, perhaps to an administrative board or a special committee of his institution. Such

[2] This wording is in no sense intended to place any additional restriction upon course exchange. It is not difficult to conceive of special cases in which the course exchange is desirable principally because the course on another campus is virtually the exact equivalent of a course on the home campus, as when a student already enrolled in one "significantly different" exchange course might, at great convenience to his schedule, enroll in a second course on the other campus simply because it was *not* significantly different from the one at his home institution. Instances like this should be left to the common sense of the adviser and the student.

"appeals"—one hopes they would be few—might have the hidden benefit of promoting among all parties an awareness of the program at another institution and a clearer understanding of the objectives of the program at the home institution.

If the opportunity for course exchange is to be used as fully and as wisely as possible, the advisory process should approach as nearly as possible that level of information, rationality, and freedom from arbitrariness which characterizes its operation for courses at the home institution. Since decisions on exchange courses are necessarily more difficult, perhaps all registration for exchange courses should be conducted one week before the regular registration, when advisers are less burdened and hurried.

Without question, the most successful arrangements for course exchange can be worked out if departments at different institutions will meet to share information and establish procedures for consultation and the advising of students. This has happened on a limited scale with some departments at some institutions. Much more could be done without unreasonable demands on time if the will to do so were more active.

D. Possible Future Concerns

If the present problems in course exchange are primarily those of removing unnecessary or irrational barriers, the future problems may well be those of establishing reasonable limits.

No institution or teacher need fear that encouraging greater opportunity for student exchange will swamp its facilities or overwhelm his classes. A very simple remedy can be applied through establishing quotas for class size (long customary at the University and in seminars at the colleges). Within a class or seminar a quota can be reserved for exchange students, and selection for that quota could be made either by the teacher or by the home institutions of the exchange students.

RECOMMENDATIONS

1. **In addition to recognizing the merits of exchange courses in specialized fields within a student's major which are not available on his own campus and of courses in an appropriate discipline which may not be represented at all on the home campus, the five colleges should recognize the value of an exchange course which offers a significantly different educational experience to the student even in a subject which overlaps a course available on the home campus. Where a proposed exchange course makes reasonable academic sense for a student's program, the five colleges should also recognize the merit for a student's educational development of gaining some experience of a different educational atmosphere.**
2. **The existing catalogue statement governing the policy for course exchanges should substitute the phrase "if the course is significantly different from any available to him on his own campus" for the present wording, which says "if the course is not available to him on his own campus."**
3. **Each institution should establish some process by which a student and his adviser can gain further information on a proposed exchange course. The student should be allowed to present his case to higher authority if this information-gathering process does not resolve a disagreement.**
4. **Greater efforts should be made to make available information on courses at all the institutions in**

the form of syllabi, reading lists, and course critiques.

5. Preregistration for exchange courses should be conducted in a specified period before regular registration periods at the five colleges, or the period for dropping and adding courses should be extended.
6. Departments at the five colleges should be encouraged to share information on their courses and establish procedures for advising and admitting exchange students.
7. There should be a continuing effort among the five colleges to make as nearly simultaneous as possible the opening and closing of the academic year, the examination periods which close each term, the advising and registration periods, and the time of appearance of course catalogues.
8. Five-college guidelines should be established to govern the setting of quotas for exchange students in classes likely to be oversubscribed.

IV

The Four-One-Four Calendar

A PROPOSAL FOR A COMMON CALENDAR WITH A JANUARY TERM PLANNED FOR CONSCIOUS COMPLEMENTARITY AMONG THE FIVE COLLEGES

THE FULLER POSSIBILITIES of five-college cooperation can be achieved only in a situation which reduces the inherent difficulties of exchange, which emphasizes the particular strengths of each institution while making these available to others, and which encourages imaginative planning of cooperative educational enterprises. One thoroughly feasible institutional change promises to achieve all these effects. It is a program which has been adopted by a growing number of college consortia—many of them less favorably situated than our own five colleges to take advantage of the opportunities created. It is a kind of program which has already appealed to many in our separate institutions but which has never before been seriously considered by them as a joint venture with all of the added dimensions possible through five-college cooperation. The members of the Long Range Planning Committee are unanimously convinced that the five colleges should move to a common Four-One-Four calendar (four months—one month—four months) and should plan for a January term to include forms of educational experience not ordinarily available as well as forms of five-college cooperation not ordinarily possible.

It has long been argued that more closely coordinated calendars at the five institutions would facilitate cooperation. Likewise, most of the faculties have separately considered—and one has attempted—some form of interim term during which students could undertake and teachers could offer diverse patterns of education not feasible within a customary semester. The apparent advantages have not yet seemed sufficient to produce any lasting change in the five separate calendars.

The LRPC is convinced, however, that fresh and compelling reasons now exist for moving toward a common calendar with a January term for educational experiments and for greater cooperative opportunities. The growing number of students taking exchange courses and the further growth of cooperative activities envisioned in this report make coordination of the five college calendars more urgent than ever before. The increasing demands of many students and some faculty for a greater range of educational experiences point to the value of a January term for testing the merits of some educational experiments while preserving the integrity of the more traditional semesters. The enhanced possibilities for conscious complementarity and cooperation among the five colleges during a term when the difficulties of transportation, class schedules, and customary routines would be greatly lessened provide a final fresh and persuasive reason for serious consideration of this proposal. The colleges should be informed by historical experience on this matter but not bound by it.

A. History of Proposals for a January Term

According to a recent historical study of nationwide experiences with an interim term,[1] the original idea for such a term was conceived within the Valley institutions. In 1958 the four-college committee planning "New College" proposed a January term "when everything will be different." The idea immediately attracted favorable attention, and within a few years colleges from Maine to Florida had instituted different versions of a January term. Meanwhile, the Valley institutions began a process of largely abortive proposals and experiments with the idea.

In 1959 a curriculum committee at Amherst proposed the adoption of a Four-One-Four calendar with an interim term during which students could pursue varieties of educational experience not otherwise available to them at that time. After some deliberation, the Amherst faculty voted down the proposed calendar. Two of the chief adverse reasons which emerged in the faculty debate were the fears that an interim term at Amherst alone would seriously handicap four-college cooperation and that departments with few majors would be hurt by a proposal which stressed specialized work within a student's major field as the primary activity during the interim term. The first of these objections would clearly not apply to this present proposal, and the second need not apply to an interim term conceived with different emphases.

[1] John M. Bevan, "The Interim Term: Its History and Modus Operandi" (mimeographed article available at the Office of the Registrar, Amherst College, where a further extensive bibliography of studies on this subject is also available). Professor Bevan is at the University of the Pacific.

Further confirmation that this idea effectively originated with the local *New College Plan* comes through correspondence with Charles E. Angell, who is completing a dissertation for the University of Arkansas on the origin and development of *Four-One-Four* calendar programs.

Smith experimented with an interim term in 1962, 1963, and 1964. During the third year, the Smith faculty in a close vote decided to conclude the experiment. Designed primarily to free students for a month to pursue whatever intellectual activities they might prefer when all obligations were removed, the Smith experiment foundered on the inability of many students to employ their freedom constructively without greater guidance. Again this experience did not conclusively prove the limitations of an interim term which might be constructed along different lines.

Still attracted by the original proposal in the *New College Plan,* Hampshire College has felt the advantages of a January term to be so important as to outweigh the obvious difficulties such a calendar at Hampshire could now create for students taking five-college exchange courses—even though exchange courses are to play a very significant role in Hampshire's plans.

The University of Massachusetts Faculty Senate is presently considering the possibility of inaugurating an interim term by reducing a student's fall semester to four courses, giving one course during the month of January, and maintaining the present five course load for the spring semester. The proposal does not spell out very fully or specifically the possibilities for using the interim term, since its sponsors decided first to ask for a vote on its feasibility. More important, the present University proposal does not consider in any way the possibilities of five-college cooperation in an interim term.

After reviewing the fates of these proposals and experiments extending back for over a decade within the institutions, the LRPC is not persuaded that this history proves either the impracticality or the lack of educational value in a January term which would be conceived from the beginning as an enterprise with five-college dimensions. Many developments within the last five years and even more developments foreseeable in the future point logically toward the creation of a January term for the five colleges. The

LRPC therefore urges that this subject be given very high priority in the deliberations of the proposed Five College Academic Policy Advisory Council.

B. Reasons for Adoption of a January Term for the Five Colleges

AMONG AMERICAN COLLEGES and universities there is now a body of experience and a range of actual enterprises which were not available for the consideration of earlier planners. Over one hundred and fifty colleges now have adopted an interim term between the longer fall and spring semesters, and other colleges have such a term under study.[2] Much evidence suggests that the sharp rise in the number of such programs is a result of the enthusiasm of both students and faculties where such programs have been tried. Moreover, these programs seem to have special advantages when they are planned by the member colleges of a consortium like that of the five colleges. Far more evidence is now available than ever existed before for the thoughtful planning of a common January term with five-college dimensions.

A January term seems ideally suited to accommodate the kind of educational experiences which are now being urged upon the colleges with increasing fervor and conviction. The current generation of college students also seems more likely than its predecessors to take advantage of these opportunities in serious and creative ways. Within a January term numerous possibilities exist for educational procedures which

[2] The member colleges of the New Hampshire College and University Council will move to a common calendar with an interim term in 1971. Their study of similar programs elsewhere, *Decade for Decision,* has informed the present discussion. A national conference on Four-One-Four programs was held in 1968, and another is planned for this year.

otherwise would not seem feasible or would interfere unduly with the procedures of a longer term. A special one-month period opens the way for many students to experience earlier in their college careers the more independent, intensive, uninterrupted study of a particular subject now possible for only a small number of advanced students. It makes possible projects which link academic knowledge with some actual experience in the field. It enables students to study and perhaps live on another campus for an easily manageable period. It frees faculty members who may desire to teach briefly on another campus. It facilitates the otherwise very difficult process of student and faculty exchange with Negro colleges which many approve in principle but find very complicated to arrange. It allows colleges to bring to a campus experts in fields where the number of scholarly professionals is still limited (as in the case of Black Studies). It encourages the close, concentrated study of some specific social problem which might be considered too special for an ordinary course. It leaves time for a carefully planned program of study in a foreign country. It greatly eases the problem of bringing outside artists, scholars, intellectuals, or foreign visitors into a context where they may provide an intensive period of lectures, seminars, or consultations with students.

Many colleges also find it possible to grant part of the faculty a full six weeks of free time for their own pursuits by combining the Christmas vacation with leave during the January term. The possible ways of enriching and intensifying the normal educational experience for both students and faculty are still being explored through experimentation with a January term at increasing numbers of colleges throughout the nation. Though some of these experiments seem faddish or superficial or more likely to evade education than to encourage it, the value of many of them for any institution willing and able to try them seriously seems evident.

At a time when the demand for untested educational innovations sometimes threatens to overwhelm the more tried and traditional procedures, the introduction of a Four-One-Four calendar also seems a responsible and conservative educational strategy. Colleges can preserve the integrity of academic work within the two four-month semesters while employing the January term to explore the educational values of some alternative procedures. The experimental programs possible in this term will help to expose both the merits and the weaknesses of innovations now passionately debated on abstract grounds.

Finally, the imaginative planning of a January program with five-college dimensions seems particularly capable of enhancing the special strengths of each institution while increasing an awareness among students and faculty alike of the full range of educational resources available in the Valley. During a January term each institution could be expected to develop, both for its own students and for interested exchange students, programs which grew from the special capacities of its faculty, students, and facilities. At the same time some faculty members from different institutions might combine to develop joint courses or programs of study in ways which prove impossible under ordinary circumstances.

Many of the practical problems in five-college exchange would also be reduced. Without the usual obligations of multiple scheduled courses each day, a student could easily undertake concentrated work in one field at a neighboring institution free from worries about coordinating the transportation system with a crowded class schedule on several campuses. Even residential exchanges for one month might be arranged for students whose interests led them to a special program being offered on a neighboring campus.

The full possibilities of a January term within the context of serious five-college cooperation have not yet been explored. The experience and the projected plans of multiple-college consortia elsewhere indicate that this cooperative aspect adds a particularly promising dimension to any

January-term program. Certainly difficulties would be involved and some sacrifices would have to be made. The potential advantages for a January term conceived on this basis, however, now seem more than sufficient to outweigh the foreseeable difficulties. Moving toward a common Four-One-Four calendar would not merely make the growing process of exchange within the longer semesters more practicable; it would also open up during the January term opportunities for educational cooperation which should prove interesting indeed.

RECOMMENDATIONS

1. **The five institutions should adopt a common Four-One-Four calendar (four months-one month-four months) and plan for a January term to include forms of educational experience not ordinarily available as well as forms of five-college cooperation not now possible.**
2. **This common calendar should be adopted after the Five College Academic Policy Advisory Council has investigated the experience and the plans of other consortia concerning cooperative plans for an interim term and submitted to the five faculties for action a full report proposing a cooperative plan for programs appropriate to the five colleges during a January term.**

V

Supplementary Academic Activities

A. Programs for Disadvantaged Students

All five institutions have demonstrated a growing awareness of the importance of including larger numbers of disadvantaged students, particularly blacks, in total enrollments. In part this has been a response to a national movement and demonstrates a partial acceptance of the concept of a more representative constituency. In part it has been a recognition that white students must be educated about the problems of race and poverty if they along with the black students are to become constructive forces in the shaping of societal change. As the institutions have increased their enrollments of black students, they have also come to realize that many of these students have never before lived closely among whites and that most of the whites have never lived in close and equal relations with any significant number of blacks. This creates special problems for individuals as well as for the institutions.

These problems notwithstanding, each institution has expressed its concern and has launched programs aimed at increasing its number of black students and providing the necessary financial aid and other assistance for them. These efforts date back to the early 1960's when recruitment visits to predominantly black schools were begun. Subsequently Mount Holyoke and Smith became founding members, together with thirteen other colleges, of the Cooperative Program for Educational Opportunity. This program was designed to identify and encourage high school students who, though qualified for challenging college opportunities, might otherwise be discouraged from applying. Other efforts in the Valley included special programs which brought groups of disadvantaged students to campus for a weekend, a colloquium for counselors who work with black students, the publication of special recruitment materials of interest to black students, and the waiving of application fees.

These efforts have recently been intensified, and all institutions have made additional financial commitments both to scholarship programs and to summer programs (discussed in Section V.C). One of these programs has been specifically designed to facilitate the admission of higher-risk students. Last year the Presidents appointed a Five College Committee on Social Responsibility, and each of the campuses created its own mechanism for studying the question and developing action programs. The University's Committee on the Collegiate Education of Black Students (CCEBS) included black members of the faculties of the other colleges.

Despite these efforts, only a small percentage of the student population in the Valley can be described as disadvantaged. Though still relatively few in number, these students, especially the black students, have made an impact out of proportion to their number on all the campuses. Many of them identify with the black power movement; some are drawn toward separatism rather than assimilation; and all have shown a pride in race as well as a concern for those reforms which seem necessary to them. Afro-American societies are gaining in strength and numbers. There is pressure for institutional change, for curriculum offerings in Black Studies, for more black faculty, for the admission of more black students, and for means to change the attitudes of some of the whites at our institutions. The colleges have responded in numerous ways, but there is no question that as more black students are enrolled, the need for change and the pressures for change will focus even more sharply upon a number of issues. One of these issues, the establishment of Black Studies programs, is discussed in Section II.A of this report.

The colleges and the University are committed to increasing still further the number of students from disadvantaged environments and to providing the necessary programs which will make it possible for these students to succeed academically and to find their roles in a changing but predominantly white environment. It is assumed, therefore, that the five institutions will continue to encourage and support programs on behalf of disadvantaged students; that the financial assistance needed to enroll a greater number of disadvantaged students will be provided; that tutorial and other ancillary services will be needed for the education of many of these students; and that conscious means for changing some racial attitudes will be explored.

Given these assumptions, the LRPC sees both economic and practical advantages in a five-college approach to attaining the objectives implied. It believes that much more effective use of combined resources can be made on behalf of disadvantaged students if more cooperation in the planning and implementation of programs is undertaken. Furthermore, the impact of such a cooperative program will undoubtedly be greater than that of individual institutional programs.

RECOMMENDATIONS

1. **A new Committee for Educational Opportunity should be appointed to replace the present Five College Committee on Social Responsibility. Its membership should include faculty members, administrators, and students from the five colleges who are qualified by position and experience to carry out the functions listed below.**

2. This committee should serve as a clearinghouse for information about programs for the disadvantaged on all five campuses; it should be consulted prior to the establishment of individual institutional programs; and it should consider, evaluate, and propose, where appropriate, joint programs:
   - for assisting admissions officers in the recruitment of disadvantaged students with the express purpose of increasing the number reached;
   - for defining admission criteria for high-risk students;
   - for developing a five-college summer program to facilitate subsequent matriculation of more high-risk students than the three private colleges are currently admitting;
   - for soliciting funds, in cooperation with institutional Development Officers, to finance programs developed and to provide supplementary financial aid for increased numbers of disadvantaged students enrolled;
   - for developing four- or five-college tutorial and counseling services to assist institutions to recognize and provide for the needs of their disadvantaged students (a coordinator-trainer might be jointly financed by four or five colleges to give advice and provide training for those involved in the individual campus programs);
   - for proposing and developing programs to assist the white members of the five-college community to recognize and act upon attitudes and practices which require change.
3. Because the implementation of the above recommendations requires some committee staff services in addition to the coordinator-trainer mentioned above, additional staff should be provided to the Five College Coordinator.

B. A Field Office for Urban & Regional Studies

NEARLY ONE HUNDRED courses on subjects related to urban life are now offered in the four operating colleges. Some fifty scholars attract several thousand students each year. The curriculum proposed for Hampshire College promises to add substantially to these figures. Many of these undergraduate courses, as well as degree programs at the University and emerging interdisciplinary areas of study, will increasingly require basic fieldwork. Some of the courses now include limited field assignments, but in general, faculty members find that they are not equipped to develop assignments which give students first-hand experience with the subject under study. The Long Range Planning Committee found almost unanimous agreement among faculty members with whom they talked that pertinent course work in the social sciences, natural sciences, and the humanities would be greatly strengthened by bringing the student face to face with the phenomena being studied. Visitation, observation, and participation in urban life at all levels, however, require preparation and negotiation within the area itself which most faculty members cannot provide without assistance.

The Connecticut River Valley from Springfield to Greenfield contains nearly all the major tensions and complexities of urban and suburban growth and management customarily associated with major metropolitan areas. If each institution were to attempt to organize fieldwork in the area, the duplication of effort would involve substantial costs to the institutions and considerable irritation to the communities being studied. The LRPC concluded that a cooperative five-college facility with some professional staff would be the most efficient means of supporting the educational efforts of the institutions with maximum cooperation from the communities. It therefore proposed to the Presidents the appointment of a five-college committee to study proposals for a field facility. The committee was appointed in October, 1968. It prepared a proposal for a Field Office for Urban and Regional Studies and is now seeking funds for its creation. It has consulted interested faculty members, city officials, faculty and administrative officers from other colleges in the area, and experienced fieldworkers.

The primary purpose of the proposed field office would be to suppport undergraduate education by establishing opportunities for field visitation and field research. It is hoped that the director of the field office will be a person with experience and training in Urban Studies. His primary task will be to consult with teachers from the colleges so that they may plan for better use of the metropolitan facilities for course work. He and the office itself would be closely related to both the Black Studies and Urban Studies Councils proposed elsewhere in this report. It is intended that when students are working in the urban area, they should be under the supervision of the field office staff.

Because the five-college area is directly affected by the growth and decay patterns of the Valley, increased awareness and involvement of faculty and students in the consequent problems will be of direct benefit to the institutions. It is expected that the staff of the field office may develop opportunities for involvement which could not be developed by the faculty members individually.

A secondary purpose of the field office will be to provide information to persons and groups in the area about educational resources and services within the sponsoring institutions which might be of value to them. It is clear that groups of interested citizens are increasingly turning to centers of higher education for consultation and training aimed at the problems with which they are struggling. Any five-college facility in the Greater Springfield area will attract inquiries from persons needing information about the resources available in the colleges. The LRPC believes that the colleges must increase their capacity to deal with such concerns.

It is hoped and expected that in time the five initiating

institutions will be joined by other institutions of higher education which also wish to make use of the facilities of the field office. Eventually, predoctoral and postdoctoral research might be based there.

RECOMMENDATION

High priority should be given to obtaining the funds with which to establish a Field Office for Urban and Regional Studies.

C. Summer Programs

A POTENTIAL METHOD of increasing the effective use of institutional resources lies in the cooperative operation of selected summer programs. The apparent economic benefits of so-called "year-round" operation may not prove to be real once careful study is made of the total costs involved; nevertheless, there may be certain programs where the social, public, and educational advantages could offset the costs. Cooperative arrangements can facilitate such programs.

The only regular college-level summer programs now offered in the Valley are the University's academic Summer Session program, the School of Social Work and the M.A.T. programs at Smith, and the Special Institute for Teachers of English in Secondary Schools at Amherst.

Mount Holyoke has had for some years, and Smith recently, a special summer program for disadvantaged students. In the summer of 1969, Mount Holyoke is running a College Bound program for eleventh-grade students, in addition to its ABC program for students from disadvantaged areas. Amherst and Smith are operating a joint "bridge program" for disadvantaged high school students preparing to make the transition to college, with Mount Holyoke undergraduate tutors participating. In addition, Amherst and Smith conduct their own ABC program. The University is conducting a bridge program for their Upward Bound high school graduates scheduled to go on to college in the fall.

Hampshire College is planning to conduct, beginning in the summer of 1971, Institutes for intensive training in foreign languages. Summer workshops in the natural sciences for promising high school and preparatory school students are also under study at Hampshire.

Most of the campuses are used during part of the summer for Alumni Colleges, and the Mount Holyoke campus is used by children from a day camp program in Holyoke. The Amherst-Smith Summer Theater is active, and various NDEA Institutes are in operation on several of the campuses. The University Conference Office conducts summer institutes and conference programs, and occasional conferences and professional meetings are held on the other campuses. Although in many cases these meetings are not run by the colleges themselves, they do make use of the campus facilities.

The new University Campus Center provides a major facility in the Valley especially designed for continuing education. It may be that facilities on other campuses as well could contribute to an effective summer program of educational service.

Although the possibilities of joint summer programs have not been discussed by the Long Range Planning Committee in any detail, the Committee believes that the opportunities warrant closer study and consideration. Among the issues that deserve evaluation are the following:

1. Facilitating the use of faculty from all the campuses by those institutions conducting summer programs of various types;
2. Offering joint programs for additional or special training in subject matter areas for secondary school teachers, especially those from urban areas (Smith College is sponsoring a program for twenty social

studies teachers on "The Black Experience—A Comparative Study: the United States and Latin America" under a grant from HEW); or conducting special programs for community college teachers;

3. Jointly planning and operating NDEA Institutes, Peace Corps Training programs, summer internships in education administration, or programs under the Education Professions Development Act;
4. Running special summer programs for area residents and others in such fields as world affairs, urban problems, and regional planning and conservation;
5. Cooperating in summer study abroad programs, which could reinforce cooperative programs in Area Studies within the five colleges;
6. Developing a five-college summer arts program for students, with cooperative events in fine arts and concerts which would also benefit area residents and serve as a supplement to programs of teacher training. (Elsewhere in this report it is recommended that two Arts Councils be established with the charge, among other things, of suggesting ways to develop the Summer Arts Program);
7. Considering the feasibility of cooperative efforts in the area of programs for disadvantaged students where each institution is already engaged in a variety of summer programs of somewhat different kinds;
8. Assessing the costs and the benefits of summer programs of appropriate types.

RECOMMENDATION

A committee should be appointed to study and report to the institutions on the possibilities of cooperative summer programs. It should establish a clearinghouse for information about summer programs and events on individual campuses.

D. Continuing Education

CONTINUING EDUCATION may be defined as a variety of forms of organized instruction designed to supplement or continue education beyond the more traditional formal systems of schooling. It tends to serve those other than regularly matriculated young students, for example, precollege youth, alumni, gainfully employed adults, and retired persons. It can take the form of short courses, institutes, conferences, evening classes, special seminars, and professional refresher training; or symposia, lectures, concerts, and panels on public issues or cultural events of general interest.

The need for continuing education has long been recognized but has not led to the development of adequate programs by institutions of higher education. Even among institutions which have responded to the need, there has been a failure to marshal the full educational resources available or to evolve a comprehensive program leading to clearly defined individual educational objectives.

There has been some recognition in the Valley of the need for continuing education programs. Forty years ago, formal cooperative efforts among the institutions were begun under the auspices of the State Department of Education, which included work with Holyoke Junior College and extension courses at Westover Field. This arrangement ended, however, in 1958.

In 1956 the *Report of the Committee on Cooperation* recommended that the colleges study the possible need for continuing education in science, in which they had laboratories and staff otherwise not readily available in the area, but the proposal was not followed up.

None of the institutions now offers a comprehensive program of adult education, although the University through the Cooperative Extension Service offers a variety of programs in agriculture, home economics, youth services, and related areas. The Labor Relations and Research Center of the University also offers short courses and institutes to members of the labor movement. In addition, various departments from time to time conduct special forms of adult education offerings. None of this, however, is operated on a general institution-wide basis nor through organized cooperative effort with the other colleges.

The Long Range Planning Committee has not discussed continuing education in detail, but believes that it is an area worth careful study. Undoubtedly, the bulk of adult education courses will continue to be offered by the state colleges, community colleges, and private institutions located in the Springfield-Holyoke area. But there may well be special opportunities for the five-college community to cooperate in particular kinds of courses for special groups; especially if they become more involved with the problems of the cities.

Several possibilities are worthy of study. The obligation of the institutions to use their special resources for service to the community, particularly the urban community, could be met by training programs for teachers and teaching assistants, special programs for the continuing education of women, and the development of unique forms of degree programs geared to the different needs of adults rather than of youth. Continuing education opportunities for members of our staffs could be provided in subjects such as computers and other electronic media, academic administration and management, technical training, and general career improvement. A survey of possibilities should include, in addition, prospects of cooperative programs in Black or Afro-American Studies, Urban Studies, Environmental Problems, and professional refresher or retraining programs.

The extensive potential of continuing education is a complicated area of educational endeavor, and the LRPC has been unable to do full justice to it. The Committee is, however, strongly impressed with its importance and therefore urges that it receive careful assessment.

RECOMMENDATIONS

1. A five-college committee should be established to consider joint action in continuing education, including recommendations of necessary steps for implementation.
2. The alumni directors should jointly study and report on the possible establishment of cooperative programs of continuing education for alumni, either held on campus in connection with reunions or summer programs, or in selected places around the country.

VI

Coeducation & Cooperation

A. The Pressures on the Colleges

THE THREE SINGLE-SEX COLLEGES in the Valley are all under pressure to adopt some form of coeducation. Student proposals range from increased five-college cooperation and student course exchange through increased residential exchanges to full coeducation. Individuals and committees at all three colleges have been studying the implications and feasibility of these proposals. The decisions of other colleges such as Yale, Wesleyan, Princeton, and Vassar have lent additional urgency to these studies, since it is possible that the actions of these institutions may have a negative effect on applications and enrollment here. More important, it is increasingly argued that there are significant educational reasons for coeducation, that classroom performance and curriculum as well as social life are improved by the presence of both sexes.

One of the most important questions to be considered by the Valley colleges in their examination of the question of coeducation is the extent to which increased five-college cooperation might enable the single-sex colleges to provide at least some of the presumed advantages of coeducation without having either to decrease the number of students of one sex whom they admit or to add a significant number of students of the other sex. A second important question is the extent to which five-college cooperation might help any college which decides to become coeducational to make the change at the least possible academic and financial cost. The third question to be considered is the possible effect on the whole cooperative program if one or more of the single-sex colleges does choose coeducation.

B. The Role of Cooperation

THE SINGLE-SEX COLLEGES believe that segregation by sex offers certain benefits to their students. There is some evidence, for example, that women are more likely to choose majors in certain fields such as science or mathematics if they do not have to compete with men. Women in women's colleges may also have more opportunity to serve in top leadership positions in student government, newspapers, and other student organizations. Could these benefits be maintained while some of the benefits of coeducation were also provided?

The most serious argument in favor of coeducation is that a majority of students of both sexes and many faculty members, especially in the humanities and social sciences, believe that the presence of both men and women in the classroom improves the quality of class discussion. Five-college cooperation can help to provide this benefit. With an increase in student exchange stemming from liberalized regulations, improved transportation, the opening of Hampshire College, and increased participation from the University, more upper-level courses and seminars can be expected to include both men and women. Even for introductory courses, most of which are offered on all campuses and therefore are not open under present regulations to exchange students except under special circumstances, agreements could be made between departments to exchange a certain number of students in order to have both sexes in classes where this is considered to be an important benefit. This arrangement would demand greater coordination of offerings and greater cooperation between departments than now exists in most cases. In addition, because of the number of women at Smith and Mount Holyoke compared to the number of men at Amherst, such a procedure would necessarily involve more exchange of male University students than presently exists.

Other suggestions designed to encourage coeducational classes are mentioned in the section of this report dealing with student exchange. Possibilities include further development of interdisciplinary and interinstitutional academic programs in which a student's whole program for a semester or a year would be planned with exchange in mind; the Four-One-Four semester schedule in which students could take January-term courses at any one of the five institutions; and increased use of semester or year exchange among the institutions in the Valley as well as among the group of eleven single-sex colleges in New England which agreed in 1969 to a limited exchange of residential students.

In addition to having students of both sexes in the classroom, both men and women students would like to have easier informal meetings which are not dependent upon the formality of dating. Residence exchanges might facilitate this, but it would be difficult to arrange a number of exchanges large enough to have a significant impact on most of the community. There are other ways in which five-college cooperation might be developed to make such contacts easier. Increasing the information available to students about events on all the campuses might help; it has been suggested, for instance, that the Five College Calendar should be distributed to all students, and that it should be issued more frequently so that it can be more up-to-date. More could be done by students themselves, with faculty and administration support, to form extracurricular clubs and associations on a five-college basis, as discussed in the section of this report dealing with student life. One of the obvious problems has been the difficulty in transportation and communication among the colleges and the University. As this improves, cooperation should be facilitated for extracurricular as well as academic activities.

The Long Range Planning Committee is aware that there have been many conversations among individuals from all five institutions on the subject of coeducation and believes that such conversations are essential and that they should be encouraged and continued. It would be extremely wasteful for each institution to repeat all of the studies that are being done. General information on the desirability, feasibility, and costs of coeducation should be shared. In addition, more cooperative thinking needs to be done on the question of distinctive forms of coeducation which might be developed through five-college cooperation.

While the Committee recognizes that each of the single-sex colleges must decide for itself whether or not to introduce any of the various forms of coeducation, it is important for all three of these colleges to recognize that their actions will affect the other institutions with which they are affiliated. Therefore, the LRPC urges that no one of the colleges make final decisions in this area without prior consultation with the other four, in order that they may consider such possible effects when making these decisions.

Further, all five institutions should cooperate to assist the others in maintaining or introducing whatever pattern each chooses. If one of the single-sex colleges should choose to adopt coeducation, five-college cooperation could help it to do so. Most women's colleges contemplating coeducation are concerned, for example, that they might not attract, at least in the first few years, male candidates of the same caliber as their female students. Because the women's colleges in the Valley are already involved in cooperative programs with a men's college and with two coeducational institutions and exchange a considerable number of students, they should experience less difficulty in recruiting good male students. It should also be possible for the recruiting and admissions officers of the men's and coeducational institutions to give assistance to their colleagues at the women's colleges on procedures and standards. It has even been suggested that Amherst might for a period of time directly assist a newly coeducational Mount Holyoke or Smith to recruit male students. Cooperative use of some facilities such as athletic fields and medical services would be an obvious saving to any of the colleges choosing coeducation.

Although the LRPC sees as one of the main values of present cooperative programs that they help to provide for the single-sex colleges some of the advantages of coeducation, the committee believes that the value of such programs would continue even if all the colleges in the Valley became coeducational. Throughout this report, the primary emphasis is on the educational value of cooperation and the ways in which it can enrich the educational programs of all five institutions. Such value is in no way diminished if all institutions are coeducational; in some fields the reasons and the opportunities for cooperation might in fact increase.

RECOMMENDATIONS

1. **All five institutions should recognize that one of the purposes of cooperation is to assist the single-sex colleges to provide for their students some of the advantages of coeducation.**
2. **Consultation and the sharing of information on the subject of coeducation should be continued as a matter of routine among the five institutions. The Presidents of Amherst, Mount Holyoke, and Smith should agree that no one of them will make decisions on or take major steps toward coeducation without prior consultation with the other Presidents. Consideration should be given by all five institutions to ways in which they might assist each other to maintain or to introduce the patterns chosen by each.**

VII
Student Life

UNTIL 1957, when qualified students were given the opportunity under certain conditions to elect exchange courses, there was little student movement among the colleges except for social engagements. Even after student course exchange was instituted, very few students attended lectures, films, or concerts at the neighboring colleges. The establishment in 1959 of a four-college transportation system did not greatly change this situation, since the buses did not run in the evening. An evening bus service among the four colleges was tried during 1965-66 but did not become established until 1967-68. The service is well patronized, and there is evidence that a significant number of students are traveling to cultural events at institutions other than their own.

In 1967 a Four College Student Coordinating Board (FCSCB) was formed on student initiative. The Board, which now consists of four student members from each institution, provides a useful forum for exchange of student views on matters of importance to them.

It is clear that most students share a desire for greater student participation in policy-making within the colleges in both social and academic areas, and would like to remove the last vestiges of the institutions' position *in loco parentis* with particular regard to parietal rules, liquor, and drugs. What appears to be critical in these issues is that the rate of change of attitudes toward them is so rapid, and intercampus communication now so easy, that the position of each institution is inevitably affected by that of the others. This being so, some conscious consultation among the five colleges appears to be essential.

The hope of the Long Range Planning Committee is that student life at the five Valley institutions will not only contribute to the education of the students but also be as attractive as that anywhere else in the country. The five institutions, one for men, two for women, one small coeducational college, and one large coeducational university, could together offer to all their students a wealth of extracurricular activities and social events impossible at any single institution. Students with common goals could come together in five-college organizations. Through interinstitutional cooperation students can enjoy both the evironment of a large university and that of small colleges.

In the total student population in the Valley there is an almost equal balance between the sexes. A significant increase in all-college social events and in the variety of joint extracurricular activities might, to a degree, satisfy the current pleas for coeducation from students in the single-sex institutions. Joint International Relations clubs, Russian Studies clubs, religious associations, and outing clubs are examples of such activities. Music, drama, and certain other groups work together, but it is surprising how little cooperation exists even in these areas. The LRPC recognizes that such cooperation must come primarily from student initiative, but believes that more faculty and administration support would be useful.

Off-campus recreational facilities for students of the five colleges are limited. Coffee houses and other facilities where students can meet informally, for example, would increase diversity in student life and contribute to a more cosmopolitan atmosphere. The five institutions need not provide all such facilities themselves, but it may be possible for them to encourage their growth.

Improvements in the transportation system, student exchange, collaboration among student governments, disciplinary procedures, drug education, scheduling cooperative social and cultural events, organizing summer programs for disadvantaged minorities, developing recreational facilities in the Valley, and coordinating community service projects all seem desirable. It is also predictable that the institutions will be obliged to develop procedures to protect the welfare of their students living off campus.

A Committee on Student Life consisting of two students and the Dean of Students from each of the five institutions was appointed by the LRPC. This committee studied the aspects of student life mentioned above, and others in which a cooperative approach did not, on examination, seem particularly promising. A number of the topics which came under their scrutiny—transportation, student exchange, cooperative summer programs, mental health services—are covered in other sections of this report, and the recommendations of the Student Life Committee were considered in discussions of those sections.

Of the subjects discussed by the Student Life Committee, three of particular concern to students were thought to be susceptible to action on a five-college basis. Disciplinary rules differ among the several colleges. As movement of students among the institutions increases, a means for clearly informing students of the rules and for enforcing them fairly should be established.

A second subject of concern was education about drugs, to enable students to make mature decisions about them. The Student Life Committee suggested that a five-college educational program, drawing upon knowledgeable people from the several institutions, could be considerably stronger than a program mounted by any single institution. This proposal, and similar considerations on education about human sexuality, are discussed in Section VIII.G on mental health services, but a specific recommendation on drugs is made here.

Student off-campus housing was a third subject of major concern. Although students are inclined to reject direction of their private lives by their institutions, many of them seem to expect to be protected from excessive rents and substandard housing when they live off campus.

The LRPC considered the general subject of housing to be of concern to the five colleges for broader reasons than those considered by the Student Life Committee. Section IX.B of this report contains the LRPC's recommendations on the broader issues. On balance, the LRPC believes that the student desire for some institutional oversight of their housing conditions should be met and accordingly includes in this section a recommendation on the subject.

RECOMMENDATIONS

1. **The Deans of Students of the five institutions should meet regularly with student representatives to consider ways of increasing student movement among the institutions and encouraging joint activities.**
2. **A five-college program of education about drugs should be initiated, and the health services should make a joint study of the subject.**
3. **The rules for student conduct on each campus and the disciplinary action that may be expected in case of violation should be made known to all students in the Valley. An attempt should also be made to have rules and disciplinary procedures as closely aligned as possible. When there is an infraction, a judiciary representative from the campus where the violation occurred should sit in as adviser to the violator's home judiciary.**
4. **A single individual at each institution should be designated to be the source of information about student housing and to work with his counterparts at the other institutions and with student representatives toward the development of a joint code for off-campus student housing consonant with existing local codes.**

5. **The five institutions should encourage public and private initiative in the development of recreational programs and facilities likely to benefit students.**

VIII

Cooperative Planning and Use of Facilities and Services

A. Rationale and Method

THE COOPERATIVE PLANNING and use of facilities and services is one of the areas in which five-college cooperation could provide not only better services, but financial savings as well. In some areas, including the sharing of library resources and, to a lesser degree, of computers, cooperation is already fairly well developed. The LRPC believes that much more extensive cooperative planning, development, and use of facilities, including buildings, could result in substantial savings to the institutions. In the past, each has tended to go its own way, with little or no consideration given to cooperative possibilities. For instance, the colleges have not consulted with each other before building new art museums, buildings for the fine and performing arts, or science facilities. With prior consultation, they might have found that some degree of specialization would have allowed each to achieve more, in cooperation with the others, than it could achieve on its own.

In analyzing the possibilities of cooperation in physical facilities, the principle must be maintained that each institution must have the facilities necessary to ensure its own academic integrity. Furthermore, it is clear that maximum opportunity for cooperative efforts in relation to facilities depends to a great extent on a workable program of cooperation in planning curriculum and academic programs.

If and when closer cooperation can be effected in curriculum planning, cooperative possibilities in planning or using physical facilities will follow more readily. Even in the absence of such cooperative curriculum development, however, the exchange of plans for physical development through the Coordinator's Office would at least alert the respective institutions to opportunities for cooperation, including exchange of ideas and experiences, which they might explore to their mutual benefit.

The LRPC, in discussing this area, found an almost total lack of knowledge among the institutions about the facilities existing among them or about plans under way or contemplated for future facilities. Three of the institutions are planning art centers. To the Committee's knowledge, very little sharing of ideas or experiences has taken place as each institution proceeded with its planning. The Physical Facilities Inventory now being compiled by the State Higher Education Facilities Commission could help to provide data in this area if the respective inventories were placed on file for exchange through the Coordinator's Office.

Once an inventory of physical facilities is available, and once the exchange of information about pending plans for new facilities is operating through the Coordinator's Office, the Committee foresees a range of potential cooperative efforts extending from simple exchange of information, experience, and design ideas, through use of facilities on another campus, to cooperative support of joint facilities.

RECOMMENDATIONS

1. **The Physical Facilities Inventory of each institution being completed for the State Higher Education Facilities Commission should be placed on file in the Coordinator's Office.**
2. **Twice annually, in January and July, the planning officers of each institution should submit to the Coordinator's Office for circulation to all other**

planning officers a report of projects in construction and of pending or planned projects, including, when possible, building programs.

3. **Each institution should make its building plans available to the Coordinator on his request, and at the expense of his Office.**
4. **Those responsible for physical facilities planning should meet at least four times a year to discuss areas of common interest.**

B. Transportation

THE LONGEST DISTANCE between any two of the five colleges is eleven miles and under normal conditions can be covered by private car in about twenty minutes. Public transportation, however, is both infrequent and much slower. Ironically, thirty or forty years ago there was better public transportation among the colleges than there is now. The trolley lines which used to connect the towns, however, were abandoned before World War II.

The 1956 *Report of the Committee on Cooperation* recognized that "one of the major difficulties in the way of cooperative action is the matter of transportation." The colleges have been grappling with the problem ever since. At first taxis were used, but as the number of students taking exchange courses increased, this became too expensive. Subsequently, two nine-passenger buses were purchased and operated on an hourly schedule. They, too, became inadequate and by 1967–68 had to be supplemented from time to time with larger chartered buses. Even so, there were times when students were left behind at one or another of the stops.

For 1968–69, the two bus companies holding the franchises between South Hadley and Amherst (Holyoke Street Railway) and Northampton and Amherst (Western Massachusetts Bus Company) were engaged to provide hired buses to supplement their existing commercial runs to give approximately hourly service during the day five days a week and three runs in the evening seven days a week. This is an interim arrangement to provide transportation while a better system is being devised. The cost for the past year was about fifty thousand dollars.

The present system, although a great improvement, is far from ideal. Hourly service is too infrequent to encourage student exchange because it usually takes a student two hours of travel time (including waiting periods) to take a one-hour class at another institution. Since there is no direct bus between Smith and Mount Holyoke, students on this route sometimes require even more travel time. This is too costly in student time and constitutes a serious obstacle to student exchange. Faculty members who are dubious about cooperative commitments often give as a reason the inadequacy of transportation.

During the hours when the buses are not running or when the schedule is very inconvenient, students travel about the Valley by hitchhiking or by using private cars. Hitchhiking is an uncertain means of transport; it is illegal and it presents considerable personal risk to the hitchhiker. Student use of private cars in the Valley has increased greatly in recent years as automobiles have become more plentiful and college rules on cars on campus have been relaxed. This adds to the problems the colleges and the community already confront in providing adequate roads and parking spaces.

Objectives

The immediate objective is to develop a system which, through a combination of bus schedules and class times, will make it possible for a student to spend no more than one hour in travel for each hour class taken at another institution. An ultimate objective is to enable students to move from one institution to another within (probably extended) class breaks. This is now technically feasible, but the cost is prohibitive.

Another objective is to facilitate student and faculty travel between the institutions in the evenings for lectures, concerts, plays, and other events so as to enable all members of the several communities to take advantage of cultural events in the Valley, to alleviate to some extent the pressures for coeducation, to facilitate the exposure of students to different atmospheres, and to enhance the sense of five-college intellectual community.

A third objective is to provide a transportation system of sufficient convenience to bring about a significant reduction in the number of automobiles traveling among the colleges and thus to reduce traffic hazards, pollution, the need for parking lots, and the pressure for generally covering the landscape with concrete.

Means

A half-hourly service should be provided among the institutions, at least during class hours. This would be possible with six buses. Four might have a capacity of twenty to twenty-five passengers, but at least two should probably have a capacity of forty-five to cover heavy runs. Total cost of the six would be about $120,000 ($15,000 each for four and $30,000 each for two).

The major component of operating cost is the cost of drivers. If student labor were used, it might be possible to operate the buses at thirty cents per mile. At about 325,000 miles per thirty-two-week year, the operating cost approaches $100,000. The possible development of a five-college motor pool to service both the buses and other vehicles is suggested by the magnitude of the operation.

The Long Range Planning Committee believes that the ultimate benefits will far outweigh the costs by removing a major obstacle, both practical and psychological, to increased cooperative programs and student exchange. The colleges should therefore be prepared to invest substantial sums of money in the improvement of the transportation system.

The problems involved in transportation are so complex that expert outside advice will be needed to solve them. The interrelationships between class schedules and optimum bus schedules, for instance, are not clear, nor are questions about flexibility of bus schedules to accommodate larger than usual numbers for certain occasions. A consulting firm with experience in systems analysis could give us invaluable help in approaching these problems. The cost of such consulting services might be fifteen to thirty thousand dollars.

RECOMMENDATIONS

1. **The colleges should recognize that improved transportation is essential to academic cooperation and that substantial annual expenditures upon it are to be anticipated.**
2. **Funds should be sought to bring in a consultant or consultants to make a study of transportation needs and to recommend ways to meet them, including consideration of a five-college motor pool to buy, service, and dispatch all vehicles, including five-college buses; and the possibilities of a student-run bus system.**

C. Computers

COMPUTERS ARE USED in colleges for research, instruction, administration, and library operations. The five colleges now have a standing committee with three subcommittees, which keep under review the possibilities of cooperative uses of computers in these areas. There has been some use of the computer facilities of one college by others, but there is still disagreement as to whether computers in the Valley should be jointly owned, managed, supported, or planned.

It is the potential economies of scale which make cooperation in uses of computers so attractive a prospect since, in general, unit costs go down as the computational load goes up. This is not always true, however, since nearly half the cost of operating any computer installation is in staff salaries for systems design and programming. It is expensive to design and program a system for one institution; when several institutions are involved they must agree on a common system or adopt an expensive system of modular programming. This may lead to the imposition of more and more restraints on system design until it becomes clear that all the conditions cannot be met or that the common system is less useful to each institution than separate systems would be. Much time may be spent in arriving at one of these conclusions. The difficulties generally encountered in trying to develop common systems are human affection for doing things one's own way and differing institutional goals, standards, staffing commitments, available capital, priorities, policies, and procedures. It thus appears unlikely that the future course of cooperation in administrative data processing will be that of common systems except with respect to new data banks for five-college purposes, such as the proposed inventory of faculty resources, for which a common system may be adopted from the start.

The immediate objective of the standing subcommittees on administrative data processing and on library computer applications is to find paths around these obstacles or to find alternate forms of cooperation. In the library area a computer-generated union catalogue of serials is scheduled for first publication in the fall of 1969. A start has been made toward forming the base for a machine-stored bibliographical catalogue, and a recommendation that the colleges establish a joint systems staff to work with the University library computer applications staff has been made by the five-college committee on library computer applications. The standing subcommittee on administrative data processing has also recommended a joint systems staff, and considerable progress has been made in devising ways in which the colleges can cooperate in the use of the Amherst IBM 1401 administrative computer.

Many of the factors which may discourage cooperation in library and administrative computer applications do not apply, or apply to a lesser extent, to research and instructional uses of computers. Typically, research applications do not affect other operations of a college, since they are designed and programmed by the researcher or his staff. Partly offsetting this simplification is the fact that research needs are not as readily predictable as are administrative computational needs. The critical questions in planning research and instructional needs are the amounts and types of service to be provided. What type of time sharing, how much batch-processing capacity, which computer languages should be supported, and how much programming support is to be available at the computing centers are among the principal matters to be decided. It may not be possible to arrive at Valley-wide estimates of need which are sufficiently firm to warrant setting up a cooperative computer center, even if the nature of needs should indicate that this should be done. At least further work in determining projections of academic research and instructional computing needs would make it more likely that the needs of all could be taken into account in the planning of each college. This would ensure that the greatest benefits would be obtained by extending the present ad hoc sharing arrangements, whereby each college permits others in the Valley to use its academic computing facilities on a favorable basis.

RECOMMENDATIONS

1. **The Five College Computer Committee and its three subcommittees on academic, administrative, and library uses of computers should continue to coordinate computer planning in the Valley through the exchange of information on institutional needs and plans. The committee should propose formal cooperative arrangements when appropriate and should encourage the fullest possible sharing of institutional computational facilities.**
2. **The four colleges should establish two systems design staffs, one for administrative and the other for library computer uses, to work with the appropriate University groups.**
3. **The standing committee should establish a means of circulating lists and abstracts of computer programs available in the Valley which are likely to be of use to others in the five-college area.**

D. Other Electronic Instructional Tools

Present Situation

In addition to computers, a number of other electronic tools might be shared for efficiency and economy. Examples are television (general educational television networks, closed circuit television, or video tape), radio broadcasting facilities, dial-access instruments which provide stored information on demand, electro-writers by which an instructor's actual handwriting and comments can be transmitted to another location, certain kinds of language laboratory facilities, and films.

Proposals made in the past for intensive study of these

instructional tools and of general communication among the institutions have not secured the necessary funding. A rudimentary inventory was taken last year by the School-College Relations Committee of facilities at the colleges, the University, and also in the Amherst, Northampton, Granby, Hadley, and South Hadley public schools. This inventory covers radio and television equipment, computers, other information-retrieval systems, data processing equipment, and high-volume duplication equipment. The inventory requires further refinement and organization, but even in its present form it suggests some areas in which resources might be shared.

During the 1967-68 academic year, the School-College Relations Committee proposed a study of needs in this area and of ways these needs might be met, but efforts to obtain funds with which to undertake the study were unsuccessful.

Objectives

Any study of the electronic instructional tools and physical facilities of the schools and colleges should consider how the institutions relate to each other academically. Hiring a consultant to tell us that the colleges can be linked by closed-circuit television, for example, does not necessarily help us decide whether they should be so linked. That depends on academic decisions about the educational values involved.

Each of the five institutions has already made commitments to some devices and can be expected to make more in the future. Future commitments should be considered collectively in order to ensure the most efficient and economical use of resources.

In order to have informed consideration of the needs and possibilities in this field, a five-college study of available electronic instructional tools and of the most effective means of using them should be undertaken by the institutions or by a responsible professional firm or individual.

RECOMMENDATIONS

1. **The Academic Policy Advisory Council should establish the priority to be assigned to obtaining a thorough study of the potential academic uses of electronic instruments to support teaching.**
2. **If the Council considers the above subject to be of high priority, a study should be launched with internal resources, by the Audio-Visual Center at the University, for example, or funds should be sought to employ a consulting firm.**

E. Libraries

SHARING OF library resources was one of the earliest cooperative ventures among the Valley institutions. An inter-library loan system was developed at an early date, the Hampshire Inter-Library Center was established, and each college extended in-person use and borrowing privileges to faculty members at the other colleges. Students taking exchange courses and certain other qualified students have also had limited in-person use and borrowing privileges.

The academic community in the Valley is now too large to permit each library to extend free service to all members of the other institutions while at the same time discharging its fundamental obligation to its own students and faculty. Hence, in recent years the number of persons given free access to the library collections has had to be restricted. Borrowing and use privileges for both faculty members and students within the five-college area are likely to become even more restricted in the future.

The Long Range Planning Committee had several meetings with the librarians and with students to discuss the problems and possibilities of library cooperation. Members of the Five College Student Coordinating Board have also met with individual librarians during the past two years. Students, of course, are interested in the freest possible exchange of library privileges; the librarians are concerned about the increasing pressures on the resources of their libraries.

The LRPC recognizes that restrictions on the use of each library by persons from other institutions are necessary but hopes that these restrictions can be as flexible and as fair as possible. The problem is to ensure access to those who really need to use another library while discouraging those who wish merely to have pleasant surroundings or social opportunities and who thus overcrowd the facilities to the extent that the library cannot adequately serve its own institution. One proposal, made by a group of students at the University and now under consideration by the librarians, is a pass system for library use. Each institution would issue a limited number of passes to another library for a particular purpose and for a limited period of time. Such a system would permit any student with a legitimate academic need to have access to the resources of the other libraries. It has also been proposed that the librarians consider a fee system for library use by both students and faculty from the other institutions. Any fee should be modest enough so that it does not thwart legitimate uses, and special arrangements might have to be made to equalize the financial burden on individual students.

No one foresees any immediate need to restrict interlibrary loan. In fact, only last spring this service was made available to freshmen and sophomores for the first time. A variety of ways are being explored to make the service more useful. With the present service, most books are delivered within twenty-four hours of the request, and the introduction of a teletype connection, a possibility which has been suggested, would not improve this much. However, better knowledge of what is available at the other institutions would greatly facilitate the service. In September, 1969, the college libraries, in cooperation with the Forbes Library and the Massachusetts Bureau of Library Extension, plan to publish the first edition of a five-college union list of serials, based on the University's *Catalog of Journal and Serial Holdings* supplemented by current acquisitions information from the other libraries. This project was approved by the Presidents upon the recommendation of the Librarians, supported by the LRPC. Initially this union list will not represent all holdings in the Valley, but it is hoped that complete information will be incorporated by the fall of 1971. The union list will be a valuable tool for faculty and students and will make it possible for the colleges and HILC to take further steps to coordinate their acquisition policies.

There have been recurring proposals to establish a comprehensive union catalogue for the five libraries. The serials catalogue represents an important step in this direction, and the librarians are considering further possibilities, but given current technology, union catalogues are expensive to establish and maintain. The Library of Congress' machine-readable catalogue record projects may ultimately bring a comprehensive union catalogue within reach.

Another way to make better use of library resources would be to divide responsibility for building collections in selected areas of learning. Basic materials would have to be held in all libraries. A division among the libraries of responsibility for holding more advanced material would include responsibilities for teaching as well as for the building of library collections. To be effective, decisions on which institution holds what would have to be made at the highest institutional level and would require strong faculty support. Decisions in the area of teaching would be particularly difficult to maintain because of the changes in student demand for courses and the changes in faculty specialties that inevitably occur among the several institutions. Division of responsibility for building collections would also be difficult in itself, since few books are sufficiently narrow and specific in their coverage to be the legitimate interest of only a very restricted specialty. Nevertheless, if it proved possible to divide academic responsibilities among the institutions, collection building responsibilities would follow with relative ease. The LRPC, however, does not now recommend that an effort be undertaken to make a specific assignment of academic responsibilities

The Hampshire Inter-Library Center

The Hampshire Inter-Library Center (HILC), established in 1951, was one of the first formal cooperative ventures among the Valley colleges. The Forbes Library of Northampton became an associate member of the Center in 1963. The participating institutions hoped that they could better serve the academic community by holding in HILC many serials and periodicals needed only occasionally at each institution and by purchasing cooperatively highly specialized books which the colleges individually might hesitate to acquire. The aims of the Center are thus sufficiently precise and limited in scope to permit a simple test for excluding titles from consideration for the collection: if two or more colleges believe that a title is important enough to their programs so that it must be on their campuses, HILC will not acquire it. It is in each institution's interest not to duplicate a title held jointly in HILC if the demand for it is not heavy on its own campus. In order to assure that the titles added will be those which are most useful to the academic programs in the Valley, there is a process of review of acquisition proposals by faculty and librarians.

Although HILC has been remarkably successful in achieving its goals, some critics claim that it no longer meets the needs of the institutions as their own collections expand. The University alone is projecting a collection of two and a half million volumes by 1980, for instance, whereas the HILC collection is only fifty thousand volumes. It has been suggested that the purposes served by the Center should be assumed by the University in the future, especially since the

University collection already duplicates a number of the titles in HILC and purchases many titles which might otherwise have been considered appropriate for HILC.

This line of argument, by concentrating upon specific titles which are bought or not bought, fails to take into account the buying policy of HILC which serves as the justification for the cooperative venture and as a guide for its operations. The policy is designed to be flexible enough to accommodate to changing circumstances. Titles are dropped or added to the college and the HILC collections depending upon judgments concerning the type, location, and extent of use they are likely to have.

The LRPC believes that HILC will continue to be useful even with the changing nature of the five-college community and that it should be continued as an independent library with the University retaining its full membership. Its functions might be expanded; it has been suggested, for example, that HILC could become the principal repository for materials in Oriental languages and non-Western alphabets, or the main location for documents of foreign governments. Financial limitations have kept the Center from seriously considering such possibilities; its limited budget may, in fact, have kept it from fully discharging its primary responsibility. The LRPC supports the efforts of the HILC Board of Directors to formulate an approach to financial support which will result in a larger budget and a more equitable assessment of dues.

Cooperative Use of Computers

Libraries are entering an era in which the computer will become a major tool for improving efficiency and service. Library computer applications can be divided into two groups. The first group consists of applications designed primarily to improve or replace manual systems now in operation; the second, of applications associated with new or significantly transformed services. While the two are not mutually exclusive, the distinctions between the types of application are of considerable practical importance to planners.

Applications to improve current operations represent fairly straightforward transfers of standard computer techniques to many of the clerical functions of the library, including ordering, receiving, circulation, catalogue card production, and the like. These applications generally share the following characteristics: (1) they use relatively small data bases; (2) they are likely to result in some form of cost savings or in improved service; (3) they are feasible given the present state of technology, librarianship, and programming arts; (4) they entail little or no change either in the relationship between the library and its users or in the conception of the library's place in a college; and (5) they are unlikely to require substantial changes in library procedures.

Applications of the second type include extensive on-line machine form catalogues and most forms of information retrieval, and generally involve the following characteristics: (1) they require very large data bases; (2) they may raise costs, since new services are being provided; (3) they are not generally feasible given current technology, librarianship, and programming arts; (4) they are likely to alter in important ways the conception of what a library is and how it should be used; and (5) they will probably require some form of interinstitutional cooperation, perhaps on a national level, to make them possible.

The appropriate strategy, given these differences in types of computer applications, would seem to be to proceed at once with those applications designed to improve current operations while deferring firm commitments to undertake applications of the second kind. Decisions to undertake applications requiring large bibliographic data bases must await further developments. In the meantime the colleges should not by inaction now compromise their ability to undertake such applications later. Specifically, no opportunity to record bibliographic data in machine-readable form for items in the collection should be lost if the cost of recording it is reasonably low. Several of the colleges now record in tape form the Library of Congress card numbers of items which they add to their collections. This will facilitate construction of a machine-form catalogue at a later date.

The best approach to applications of computers to current operations would probably be through two separate but coordinated computer groups, one attached to the University and one to the college libraries. The disparities in size and complexity of the operations of the University library on the one hand, and of the libraries of the colleges on the other, suggest that it will be simpler for each group to decide what needs to be done for its type of operation and then to confer on how the two systems may be made compatible. The goal of compatibility between systems, particularly with respect to the recording and handling of bibliographic information, should be given high priority, so that future development of a cooperative machine-form data base will not be hampered by insufficient forethought.

The libraries of the University and Hampshire College are now attempting to automate their clerical routines using compatible systems. The further these two libraries progress in devising mutually satisfactory computer applications, the more difficult it may be to achieve full compatibility among all the Valley libraries at a later time. Therefore, the LRPC strongly urges the four colleges to establish a joint library systems and procedures group as soon as possible. It would appear to be to each institution's immediate interest to automate some clerical functions in the libraries now in such a way as to facilitate eventual five-college cooperation and the introduction of new services as developments in technology make them feasible.

RECOMMENDATIONS

1. **HILC should be continued as an independent library. The Board of Directors should continue its study of ways in which the Center's budget**

might be increased and dues be assessed more equitably. The Board should also review functions which might be added to those now performed by HILC should additional funds be provided.

2. The Librarians of the five colleges should consider instituting a fee and/or pass system whereby each library would grant in-person borrowing and building use privileges to a limited number of faculty and students from the other four institutions.
3. The Librarians of the five colleges should be supported in their project of expanding the union list of serials now in preparation so that it will provide complete serial holdings information in book form. It should be issued on an annual basis.
4. The four private colleges should form a library systems and procedures group to work with that of the University library in designing compatible library computer applications.

F. Museums

THE FOUR INSTITUTIONS now in operation own art collections of varying degrees of importance, a geology museum, a museum of Americana, and a few miscellaneous collections whose value for public exhibition has not been fully assessed. Plans for future development affect chiefly the art collections, for which new or expanded facilities are planned or already under construction on the four original campuses and at Hampshire College as well. No joint catalogue of all the collections exists, and complete catalogues do not exist even on the home campus in most cases.

Objectives

The museums and other collections of the five colleges have a role to play on the individual campuses, in the life of the five institutions, and in the community. They constitute part of the resources that support the academic programs of the colleges. Collections on other campuses might enrich the learning opportunities of students at any one of the colleges. Beyond this, the collections provide an opportunity for pleasure and learning to the school children and adults of Hampshire County and the surrounding area and may be of importance to an even wider audience.

The objectives of the five colleges, within the limitations set by funds that are available or can be obtained for the purpose, are to achieve the greatest benefit, first for the academic programs and second for the community, which can come from having these resources in the Valley. If these benefits can be more effectively attained through cooperation, ways of bringing this about should be sought.

Fuller use of the collections might be attained through a broader program of consultation about exhibitions and through making available materials owned by one institution for exhibition on other campuses. If some collections or parts of collections are of potential interest or value to the Valley community, the possibility of some sort of joint operation should be explored.

RECOMMENDATIONS

1. **Existing museum collections should be inventoried, and their contents should be classified in two categories: those objects which an institution wishes to store on its own campus for exhibition and study, and those objects which, although of sufficient interest to rule out sale or discard, the owning institution would be willing to have placed under five-college operation and housed elsewhere.**

2. The directors of collections which institutions wish to continue on their home campuses should meet to discuss the possible value of such cooperative activities as a union catalogue of the collections, making portions of one collection available on loan at one of the other campuses, joint sponsorship of loan exhibitions brought in from outside the Valley, and synchronization of plans for loan exhibitions on individual campuses. The possibility that acquisition programs might involve exchanges of information and joint planning should also be explored. If, as the collections grow, policies could be developed on the extent to which individual institutions should specialize their collections, the usefulness and interest of the combined collections would be enhanced.
3. If there are collections of significance which the individual institutions prefer not to maintain and exhibit on their own, the possibility of joint exhibition should be investigated. It might prove desirable to invite representatives of the community to explore with the colleges the establishment of a Valley Museum Foundation, which would ultimately be responsible for the operation of a Valley museum or museums in which some of the collections of the five institutions might be housed.

G. Mental Health Services

In July, 1968, the Long Range Planning Committee asked the chief physicians at the colleges and the University for their views on the establishment of a centrally located medical center which would concentrate, at least initially, upon expanded mental health services, with the thought that the Center might be designed to serve the needs of the community as well as those of one or more of the five institutions. In addition to written replies from this group, members of the LRPC had several meetings with the physicians and with the chairman of a group of psychologists proposing a Comprehensive Clinical Services Center at the University.

Inquiries about the possible establishment of a community medical center with emphasis initially on mental health were occasioned by a conviction on the part of a number of the members of the LRPC that the incidence of mental and emotional disorders requiring treatment in a student population of twenty to thirty thousand may be greater than the present facilities and staffs at the various colleges can accommodate. Perhaps, therefore, the colleges should increase their sensitivity to mental disorder and broaden their responsibility for treatment. The LRPC thinks that there might be advantages in efficiency and confidentiality if a central facility for treatment of mental disorders were created. The Committee also believes that there is need for a preventive program in mental health. A comprehensive approach to both mental and physical health in the community should be a concern which the colleges and the University share.

Present Situation

The three operating private colleges and the University have quite different patterns of psychiatric services. Mount Holyoke has one full-time psychiatrist; Amherst has a part-time psychologist and part-time psychiatrist; Smith has a part-time psychiatrist and two full-time counselors, as well as the services of two consultant psychiatrists. The extent and character of the treatment furnished students by the three colleges are limited by the number and training of the staff in the different services, and the nature of the service varies with the psychiatric orientation of the director. The decision as to how the student's interest can best be served with the personnel and time available at each of the three colleges governs whether or not a student is sent home or kept in college under therapy of one sort or another. Seriously disturbed students are sent home. On occasion, however, a student may need to be institutionalized locally before going home, and it is for these cases that the three private colleges feel a need to have hospital beds available.

The University has evolved a service somewhat different from that of the colleges. The aim of the University's mental health services is a comprehensive student health program which has preventive elements. There are two levels of counseling: one by psychological counselors and, for more severe disorders, psychiatric care. There is a strong intention to provide preventive health care, but implementation is limited by the size of the staff and the rapid growth in the student population.

Community Health Center

In their letters and in discussion the consultants to the LRPC were in agreement on only two aspects of the Community Health Center proposal: the idea should be approached cautiously, and it had enough merit to warrant the creation of a committee to study the advantages and disadvantages. In analyzing the responses from the consultants, however, it became clear that the idea of a community health center should be kept separate from the mental health component. While there was some agreement that the expense and complexity of modern health care demand centralization, there was doubt that creation of a center that competes with or duplicates Cooley Dickinson and Holyoke Hospitals is justified. Furthermore, student health care has a special component in that a primary aim is to keep students from missing too much of their education. It is important that local care be readily available for minor ills that do not keep a student from his education but for which treatment would be time-consuming and inconvenient if done centrally. Therefore, the consultants suggested augmentation of the existing services but not their complete replacement.

Mental Health Center

Extended discussion with the consultants suggested that the complexity of issues involved in mental health deserved study by a special committee created for this purpose alone. The committee subsequently appointed met on several occasions and submitted a report summarizing the options it thought open to the five colleges. Its report recognizes the close relationship of preventive programs, including some which may be part of the curriculum itself, to service programs suited to a wide range of student needs. Each of these requirements is met by a distinct service. The committee offered suggestions for the way these services might be coordinated in the future.

There appear to be two possibilities for improving mental health services. The first is to improve intensive care services on a five-college basis through the establishment of a five-college "halfway house," that is, a residential facility for students too disturbed to remain in their dormitories but not sufficiently ill to warrant hospitalization and consequent absence from classes. A second possibility would be to provide staff time to explore with the Community Mental Health Organization, established under Massachusetts legislation for Hampshire and Hampden counties, the possible role of five-college participation in a community program focused on college-age youth.

The following statements on needed mental health services are based upon the report of the special committee:

Intensive Care: Consideration of student services for mental health traditionally conjures up the memory of the few people each year who suddenly and dramatically require intensive care for debilitating behavior disorder. The rate of such cases is probably no more than one in a thousand. At current levels, this is about twenty-five students per year. Such students require hospitalization for an average of three weeks.

Supportive Care: There are students whose general level of function dictates brief admittance to the infirmary for medication and rest before regular counseling can begin or while counseling or psychotherapy is in progress. The number of such students may be as high as six in one thousand, or about one hundred and fifty students per year.

Psychiatric Counseling: Some students come for counseling for conditions which they feel interfere with their proper functioning and development. These conditions may be longstanding, and the prognosis of immediate change may be poor, but the student's estimate of personal debilitation may be correct and continuing therapy may be indicated.

Personal Counseling: Some students seek help, not because their problem is one of personal maladaptation, but simply because they face a decision or series of decisions for which they do not feel equipped. The range of problems may be very great: adjustment to a roommate, the use of stimulants and depressants, questions about improving study habits and academic performance.

Human Development: Students have traditionally introduced into the life of their college those subjects for which they have felt a personal need. In our time, the focus is increasingly on the development of the human personality. Most immediately this centers on human sexuality, but there is also interest in the whole range of interpersonal relations, the use of stimulants and depressants, the definition of citizenship under a rule of law, and the manner in which personal identity is developed and maintained. Mental health services should and do participate in campus-wide preventive programs aimed at preparing students to cope with difficult life experiences in these areas.

Each of the colleges is of course aware that human development is a large component in the educational process as a whole. A number of programs in and among the colleges are specifically designed to educate students on human sexuality. Amherst, Mount Holyoke, and Smith students, for example, have participated in a series of seminars on the subject, but there is no doubt that more can be done to expand and coordinate such programs. In Section VII on student life, for example, the LRPC recommends a five-college program of education on drugs.

With the above needs in mind, the special committee suggested two possible ways of distributing the services required to meet them. One possible plan is to continue to restrict mental health services to college students, with five-college cooperation confined to particular program needs. Supportive care and most psychiatric counseling, including diagnosis and referral, would still be handled by each institution separately. Personal counseling and human development programs might be carried out both on each campus and cooperatively, in order to take advantage of the expanded facilities which cooperation would offer and to give the student more choice of counselors. The five colleges together could develop halfway house facilities and perhaps some intensive care facilities, although they would probably still depend on local hospitals for most intensive care.

The second possibility is to create a more comprehensive service. Five-college cooperation would be extended to leadership in the development of a mental health plan for the entire community. In such a program University training programs would be integrated with the services, and there could be greater emphasis on retention of disturbed students instead of reliance on parental support. Each institution would continue to provide supportive care and personal counseling, with limited psychiatric service. In cooperation with a community mental health organization, the five institutions could provide intensive care facilities, a halfway house, and staff and facilities for psychiatric diagnosis and treatment. Although each institution might continue its own human development program, a cooperative program for the colleges and the community could also be developed.

On the basis of the special committee's report and discussions with consultants, the LRPC believes that the five colleges should undertake more extensive study of possible cooperation in the field of mental health services.

RECOMMENDATIONS

1. **A committee should be appointed to determine the best arrangement for increased intensive care services for mental health and to submit a report on the feasibility of establishing a five-college halfway house to serve students for whom continued academic work is judged possible despite psychiatric disability.**
2. **One five-college representative should be appointed to explore the feasibility of five-college participation in the future efforts of the community mental health organization for the area.**
3. **A five-college committee should be appointed to recommend, in consultation with Deans of Students and with students, ways to foster human development programs, particularly cooperative programs for education on sex and drugs.**

H. Recruitment of Students

COOPERATION IN the recruitment of students has so far been very limited. The Directors of Admissions meet informally from time to time to exchange information. Mount Holyoke and Smith, as members of the Seven College

Conference, share in the services of two field representatives who encourage applications from states west of the Mississippi. For a number of years Smith and Amherst have sponsored a colloquium for secondary school guidance counselors, and last year Mount Holyoke and Amherst sponsored a conference for counselors of black students. The University once ran a computer tabulation of the qualifications of the applicants to the women's colleges. There have been a number of joint appearances at College Days in the secondary schools. An admissions officer from one institution has occasionally answered questions about another, but in no instance, apparently, has a recruiter from one institution acted as the official representative for one or more of the others.

A brochure on five-college cooperation prepared by the Coordinator for internal purposes has been distributed by several of the admissions offices to prospective students, and the Five College Student Coordinating Board is preparing a brochure which might also be useful to admissions offices, but neither is specifically designed for student recruitment.

At first sight there would appear to be considerable merit in the idea of developing closer and more cooperative ties in recruiting. As the search for talented students and disadvantaged students becomes more intense, there would probably be savings in time, money, and effort if, in the more remote or less populous parts of the country, one recruiter could officially serve all five institutions. With no greater expenditure of resources, such a coordinated program might reach a significantly larger number of localities and prospective students. Further, a recruiter familiar with the various strengths of the five different institutions might succeed in attracting to the Valley, if not to a particular institution, a student of exceptional talent with particular interests which another of the five colleges was especially qualified to nourish. The benefit to the other four colleges of such a student's presence, though indirect and perhaps small, is nevertheless real. Finally, since the admissions officers say that the existence of five-college cooperation is an advantage in recruitment, it might be useful to have a candidate being interviewed by one college also visit another. Thus, the girl who is considering Smith might well be influenced to choose Smith by the fact of her having been welcomed at Amherst and Mount Holyoke, although she was applying to neither.

Yet there are difficulties in setting up too formal a program of cooperative recruitment. One could expect that the present natural rivalries between similar institutions would somewhat abate, but the recruiters employed in the cooperative venture would probably need an indoctrination period in the admissions office of each school in order to be effective. Even if the recruiter himself found it possible to divide his loyalty three ways or five ways, there are likely to be administrative frustrations in the assignment of tasks and responsibilities to him. A corollary to this is the strain which might be put upon a cooperative system of recruitment if it were to move in the direction of becoming a cooperative system of admissions. It is not likely that the several institutions would relinquish their autonomy in selecting the sort of student—and the particular student—they choose to admit, nor does this seem necessary or even desirable. Finally, inclusion of the University in any cooperative scheme would pose problems.

RECOMMENDATIONS

1. **The Coordinator's Office should prepare a brochure on five-college Cooperation for the use of admissions offices.**
2. **The Directors of Admissions should prepare a report on the possibility of increased cooperation in recruiting.**
3. **Consideration should be given to putting colloquia for guidance counselors on a four- or five-college basis.**

I. A Five College Center

THE FIVE COLLEGE COORDINATOR and his staff are presently housed in Blair Hall at Hampshire College, since Hampshire is the most central of the five institutions. Office space and utilities are provided at no cost to Five Colleges, Inc. The Long Range Planning Committee has been able to use Hampshire's adjoining conference room for meetings and dinners every other Friday evening with great convenience. Some other meetings of five-college groups have been held there also, but the usual pattern has been to meet at one or another of the five institutions, sometimes on a rotating basis.

As Hampshire College grows in personnel and in the more intensive use of its own facilities and as five-college cooperation leads to a larger staff for the Coordinator's Office, together with more frequent meetings of five-college committees, the present arrangements will no longer prove sufficient. Adequate space will be needed to accommodate the expanded staff and functions of the Coordinator's Office. Likewise, the convenient location for five-college meetings at Hampshire College can only be used regularly if the Coordinator has facilities which he can confidently schedule for such purposes without interfering with Hampshire's own activities. The Trustees of Hampshire have generously agreed to set aside some of their land for building a Five College Center to meet these needs.

The LRPC sees real merit in the construction of a Five College Center located on Hampshire's land. It believes that the Center should be designed on a fairly limited scale but that the design should be flexible enough to allow for possible expansion to meet future needs. It should at least provide space for the Coordinator and his staff; rooms for meetings, seminars, and small conferences; and modest facilities for serving occasional meals. It might also provide an interchange point and even a garage with maintenance facilities for five-college buses.

RECOMMENDATIONS

1. Hampshire College's offer of land for a Five College Center should be formally accepted by Five Colleges, Inc., and the site should be determined.
2. A planning committee should be established to determine the functions and costs of a Five College Center and to make a formal proposal to the Presidents for its establishment and funding.

IX

Community Relations and Public Service

A. The Colleges & Their Environment

THE TOWNS OF Amherst, Hadley, Northampton, and South Hadley, which include the five colleges, are undergoing rapid changes as the result of population growth. In part the population growth is due to people moving into the area because of its attractiveness and increased accessibility because of new and better roads. In part the growth is attributable to the rapid enlargement of the University and the establishment of Hampshire College. More than in most areas, the forces for growth are relatively predictable in nature and effect.

The response to population pressure is, in simple terms, a struggle of opposing forces. At one extreme is the diehard proponent of the status quo, who wants nothing to change and marks every new house or paved street as one more step toward disaster. At the opposite pole is the developer, builder, or realtor whose sole aim is profit and who does not consider such matters as aesthetics, water purity, or noise levels worth consideration. Between these two extremes is the majority, citizens who are honestly concerned about the nature of the human environment as well as builders, developers, and realtors who have a balanced view of the nature of land development. The legitimacy of profit is recognized, but so is the need to apply criteria other than monetary gain to new development. Among those who would weigh more heavily either the need for commercial development or the need for conservation, most would agree that development and change in the area are inevitable and desirable. The differences in outlook have to do with the rate, direction, and quality of the results.

This middle group may be divided into three identifiable subgroups. In the first subgroup are the elements of town and city government that exercise certain powers of government, including application of building codes and zoning bylaws. The task of this group is to ensure, without much latitude for interpretation, that the mandates of the town, county, state, or federal governments regarding safety, orderly planning, and public health are carried out.

In the second subgroup are the energizing forces of change. These would include the realtors, developers, builders, lawyers, bankers, and businessmen, who prefer a climate of growth and prosperity for the conduct of their activities.

In the third subgroup are the concerned professionals and amateurs, including those professionals whose daily concerns are, in an academic or active sense, relevant to or directly concerned with the environment. These include scientists, such as biologists, chemists, geologists, physicists, hydrologists, and botanists; artists; architects and landscape architects; city planners; economists; sociologists; political scientists; and foresters. Among the amateurs would be members of conservation and recreation commissions, outdoor enthusiasts, and others with identifiable interests in the environment, together with a large group of thoughtful concerned citizens who wonder whether man can discipline himself not to create the conditions for his own doom in exploiting the environment.

The first subgroup, representing law, reacts to initiatives taken by the second subgroup, representing change, so the change group has the initiative and exercises it more or less in response to the opportunity for profit. The third group, citizens, may or may not be actively involved. Although the group representing law is also representative of the citizens, the citizens may find that they must assume new and more directly participatory roles in the process of change in order to understand and respond to increased initiatives—and increased pressure to go along with these initiatives—by the group which would introduce change. This suggests simply that the citizens group should organize and express its views clearly. By doing so, it may help to offset the forces for unregulated environmental change (and in many cases, deterioration) brought about by those who would use change only for profit.

The presence of four colleges and a university in the four towns is clearly a significant factor in any efforts to direct change in the environment of the towns. The institutions should help to define and clarify issues. As taxpayers and employers they have reason to voice their views on questions of environmental quality; above all, they include experts in almost every field relating to environmental matters, and should make available information which is of value to all citizens of the community.

The LRPC believes that because of their central role in Amherst and Hadley, Amherst College, Hampshire College, and the University of Massachusetts should take the initiative to form Committees for a Better Local Environment, and that Smith College, in Northampton, and Mount Holyoke College, in South Hadley, should do the same. The committees would be formed at the initiative of the colleges and would continue to include membership from them, but would draw the majority of their membership from a wide range of interests and professions to include representatives of organizations with environmental concerns as part of their general objectives (League of Women Voters, conservation commissions, *et al.*), and a lawyer and a realtor who share the aims of the group.

The functions of the Committees for a Better Local Environment would be advisory, educational, and consultative, and they would serve as coordinating bodies. Each group would list a number of persons with special competencies who would agree to contribute time and talent to the consideration of problems as they arise. Included among the consultants would be scientists, planners, architects, and others whose interests and expertise are relevant to environmental problems.

To coordinate the role of the five colleges in the formation of the local committees, and to provide a continuing coordinating group, a Five College Local Environment Committee should be formed with one representative from each institution, who would also serve as one of the institutional representatives on the committee for the town in which his college was situated. The chief role of the five-college committee, after the town groups were formed, would be to link the groups' needs to available people, programs, and resources at the colleges as problems arose on which the town group wished to take some action.

The five-college committee should not compete with existing conservation commissions or other groups interested in environmental issues. Where such groups exist, the committee might coordinate related efforts, provide expert advisers from one of the colleges, or serve in some other supportive role. In many cases, local groups would be better qualified to speak to an issue than would the five-college representatives.

The major activities of the Committees for a Better Local Environment would be educational and advisory. They might conduct educational programs in environmental matters through lectures or radio programs, written materials and colloquia. They might assist in the preparation of course materials for schools and colleges. When invited they might provide technical advice on the planning, design, engineering and scientific implications of proposed developments. On occasion they might also support or oppose developments with strong environmental impact.

The committees would meet at least monthly. In addition, individual members could accept the responsibility of attending meetings of local zoning boards, planning boards, and selectmen and reporting to their committees developments which they should consider or on which they should make recommendations.

RECOMMENDATIONS

1. **The five colleges should take the initiative in forming, in cooperation with their communities, Committees for a Better Local Environment in their respective towns, with broad representative membership.**
2. **One person from each institution who is serving on the committee for his area should also be designated as representative to a Five College Local Environment Committee which would help serve the local committees by providing information about special resources available within the five colleges, and which would coordinate the participation of the five colleges in environmental development.**
3. **The five colleges should encourage faculty and staff members to participate as individual citizens in official and unofficial groups concerned with the preservation and development of the environment.**

B. Housing

Massachusetts Housing Situation

The Governor of Massachusetts has declared that there is a scarcity of housing throughout the state. The result, in his view, is a landlord's market with many families living in substandard housing because they cannot afford the higher-priced units which are the only new units being constructed. The principal reasons for the housing shortage are increased population, land shortages, and high labor costs, land taking in the cities for highways and industrial-commercial development, and growing student enrollments in certain areas.

The Governor has recently suggested to the Association of Independent Colleges and Universities in Massachusetts (AICUM) that the member institutions should become non-profit sponsors of housing, particularly where they are major users or have consumed housing as they have taken land for expansion. Growing student enrollments, combined with student rejection of life in the conventional dormitory, adds to the statewide housing shortage. Examples are cited of three or four students pooling their resources to outbid local residents for rental housing. This often results in a general increase in rents. The relatively rapid turnover of students also results in annual rent increases substantially higher than is normal in a more stable market. Further, the influx of students aggravates the parking problem which, in turn, excites further cricitism of colleges and universities.

A recent survey by AICUM showed that, exclusive of students living at home, there were over twenty-seven thousand students enrolled in private institutions living off campus in the Boston Metropolitan area and an additional three thousand in the rest of the state. Figures were not available for students at public institutions living off campus.

Hampshire County

Fully reliable and comprehensive statistics on the housing situation within Hampshire County are not now available. Some years ago the University compiled an extensive study of its own projected needs and of the situation in Amherst. Efforts to keep this study up-to-date have not been completely successful because conditions are constantly changing. The League of Women Voters in Amherst made a study of the town's housing needs, but this is also now out of date.

There is little doubt, however, that the housing situation in Amherst has already become critical for students, for service personnel, and for the elderly. Reasonably low-cost or even moderate-cost rentals are in dangerously short supply; the price of land has risen so much that new housing is not being constructed to meet the demand; and the overflow of students and service personnel into neighboring communities like Hadley and Northampton has already served to place considerable upward pressure on housing costs throughout the area. A League of Women Voters study of low- and moderate-cost housing in Northampton confirms the existence of shortages there.

Some efforts have been made to deal with this situation. Three years ago an Interfaith Housing Corporation was formed in Amherst, including three faculty members and one administrator from Amherst College, and one former administrator from the University among its eleven directors. It has taken an option on sixty acres of land near the center of town and has concluded a partnership agreement with the Development Corporation of America (with headquarters in Boston) to develop this site, together with another one nearer the University, for the benefit primarily of service personnel and the elderly, but with the understanding that some married students may be admitted in case of vacancies. Housing at reasonable rentals can be built in Amherst only with the assistance of long-term, low-interest financing from the federal government, and that financing is not now available for student housing. In connection with this project, the Federal Housing Administration will soon complete a feasibility survey of the need for federally financed housing in Amherst.

In Northampton a housing group has been organized which depends for its resources upon the sale of shares to public-spirited citizens and uses the proceeds to purchase and rehabilitate older properties for rental or sale at reasonable rates. It has not yet been able to draw upon any government funds, and its operations are limited.

In April, 1969, a group of interested citizens convened a one-day Housing Institute in Northampton to which representatives of the five colleges were invited. The outgrowth of the institute was the formation of a steering committee on housing. Representatives of each of the five colleges also participated in subsequent meetings held by the group to discuss the formation of a nonprofit Housing Development Corporation (HDC) for Hampshire County, a measure which would require about $200,000 for initial capitalization. The HDC would appoint as staff director an expert on government programs which assist nonprofit sponsors to build low- and moderate-cost housing, facilitated by arrangements involving interest subsidization of loans. The steering committee recognizes that it will not be easy to interest such sponsors in the development of an HDC, and—as a necessary prerequisite to further action by local governments, businesses, and private sponsors—reliable housing statistics must be compiled. The five colleges have indicated their willingness to share to some extent with local businesses the $5,000 cost of a housing survey.

Role of the Five Colleges

In this situation the provisions for student housing made by each of our five institutions, especially the University, will have a significant impact upon housing in our communities. The present regulations governing off-campus living by full-time students at the existing four institutions are as follows:

The University allows all married students, graduate students, and students over twenty-one (with permission of the Dean of Students) to live off campus. The Graduate Student Senate at the University recently claimed that the University can provide housing for only nine thousand of its fifteen thousand enrolled students.

Amherst allows married students to live off campus. In 1968–69, Amherst began a new policy to allow up to a maximum of twenty unmarried students to live off campus if the reason given was sufficient to persuade the College Deans to grant approval. Only seven students availed themselves of this new option last year, but more are doing so this year.

Both Mount Holyoke and Smith allow married undergraduates and all graduate students to live off campus.

Increasing pressures for permission for undergraduates to live off campus are expected at the private colleges. In order to avoid vacant dormitory rooms, and consequent loss of revenue, the private colleges will be necessarily reluctant to grant this permission. It would be possible to resolve the problem by limiting the number allowed to live off campus and at the same time increasing the enrollment by the number so authorized. The LRPC recognizes that many factors enter into consideration of off-campus living. The Committee recommends that the impact on local housing be weighed carefully prior to liberalization of existing regulations.

It could be argued that the colleges and the University are not responsible for the housing shortage in the state or in Hampshire County. The shortage is primarily a result of the population explosion, lack of action in the past by local communities to sponsor public housing, and the effect of our present inflationary situation, which makes low-cost housing uneconomical to construct. On the other hand, it can also be argued that the colleges can use their influence to spur local effort, that they have an interest in better housing for both their employees and off-campus students, and that as leaders in areas of social concern, they should act as a catalyst in this critical area. In Amherst, and to a lesser extent in the surrounding communities, the expansion of the University has played a major role in creating a housing shortage. The town is already alarmed at rumors that the University may soon stop building any further student housing. The five colleges cannot afford to allow this situation to deteriorate further, when clear and responsible planning could improve it.

Standards for Off-Campus Housing

Students who live off campus are subjected to conditions that are often the outgrowth of any housing shortage: high rents, substandard, unsanitary units, and improper fire protection. Today's undergraduate argues that the college should not act *in loco parentis,* and college authorities are increasingly accepting this point of view, at least with respect to upperclassmen. Students also argue that as adults they should be free to live off campus and not be restricted to dormitory living. The question then arises as to what responsibility the college or university is to assume in regard to inspection of and standards for off-campus units when it is trying to avoid a parental role.

The LRPC was divided on this point. The organization and mechanics for inspection and approval of off-campus housing are costly and might soon involve the question of what is fair rent. The college could find itself involved in an argument between tenant and landlord concerning whether standards are being met. On the other hand, if students should be injured or killed as a result of fire in a substandard unit, the institutions could not escape bearing some of the responsibility. On balance, the Committee concluded that the establishment of minimum standards for off-campus housing for students should be considered by the five colleges.

RECOMMENDATIONS

1. **The five colleges should work with responsible citizens' groups which are trying to increase the availability of low- and moderate-cost housing.**
2. **Before liberalizing existing regulations, the colleges should study the availability of housing and the environmental consequences of permitting large numbers of students to live in non-college housing.**

3. The colleges should consider developing minimum standards for off-campus student housing and requiring all units to be placed on an approved list prior to rental to students.

C. Community Services

THE COLLEGES and the University both collectively and individually offer a number of services to their communities. Collectively they are the principal support of the five-college radio station, WFCR (FM), the *Massachusetts Review,* and the Five College Calendar of Events. Concerts, plays, and lectures on all of the campuses also contribute to the cultural resources of the area.

The institutions sometimes offer their facilities to individuals and groups in the community free or for a nominal fee. Permission is often granted to use recreational facilities during certain hours or during the summer.

The institutions for some years have worked with the five school districts of their area. The relations of the University School of Education with the schools are of course close, but faculty of the private colleges are also involved in a number of joint projects, and students from Mount Holyoke and Smith do practice teaching in the local schools. A formal School-College Relations Committee composed of representatives of each of the five colleges and the superintendents of the five school districts meets regularly to consider ways in which the two groups can work together to their mutual benefit.

Faculty members and students participate in a wide range of community activities, such as tutoring programs in Holyoke and Springfield, service at the Northampton State Hospital or the Belchertown School, and participation in conservation groups, housing committees, local governing bodies and the like.

The University offers a much wider range of services to the community than do the private colleges, including industrial and agricultural consulting services, adult education courses, and informational pamphlets. It has both the obligation and the resources to do so. It is clear, however, that all five institutions have a large and expanding role to play in this area.

When the Long Range Planning Committee began discussing community services, it asked each institution to list activities in which it was involved. The number and variety of activities listed was most impressive. It seems to the LRPC that an inventory of such activities and programs would be useful for several purposes. It would help students and faculty find out about programs at the other institutions in which they might wish to participate, and it would help people in the communities know where they might get assistance. Such an inventory could be compiled and kept up-to-date by the Coordinator's Office; both that office and the Field Office for Urban and Regional Studies described in Section V.B of this report could act as centers of information for the community on the services available from the colleges.

Initially, the LRPC thought that some coordination of community services among the colleges might be useful, but after consultation with the directors of several of the programs and with members of the community which they serve, we see no present desire or need for such coordination. We do believe, however, that to the extent possible, projects of one institution should be open to participation by faculty and students of another. There may be a need in the future, if community services are greatly increased, for some coordination to avoid unnecessary duplication and confusion among the programs.

RECOMMENDATIONS

1. **An inventory of community services should be compiled and maintained under the auspices of the Five College Coordinator.**
2. **Students or faculty from one institution should be able to participate in service programs of another institution whenever feasible.**
3. **Both the Coordinator's Office and the Field Office for Urban and Regional Studies should be able to give information to members of the community about the services available from the colleges.**

D. Legislative Relations

WHILE JOINT five-college activities may be warranted occasionally in regard to state legislation, the most productive cooperative efforts are likely to be in the area of federal legislation. It is at this level that the mutual interests of all institutions converge most readily upon common objectives.

Some educational consortia maintain Washington offices, but this is expensive and the benefit would have to be high to warrant the cost. The most direct benefit would come from soliciting grants and contracts, but there is little evidence to suggest that the five colleges are now missing sufficient opportunities to justify establishing a Washington office to assist them.

An alternative route to Washington representation is offered by some educational associations. The National Association of State Universities and Land-Grant Colleges, for example, offers such services on a retainer basis (for an institution the size of the University the annual fee is five thousand dollars). Again, however, the question arises of whether the returns justify the cost.

A useful approach might be to organize a means of rapid exchange among the five colleges of information about federal legislation and programs. Such an arrangement would facilitate prompt response to pending legislation and could include provision for issuing joint statements or sending joint representatives to work personally on a given issue in Washington. Other appropriate methods of cooperative action should be explored, such as a five-college meeting with congressional representatives.

The five colleges should join other institutions in seeking increased federal funding for higher education in this country. Unless all institutions of higher education are willing and able to make a strong case for improved federal support, other demands for federal funds are likely to be given precedence as funds become more available.

Mechanisms for common efforts to prevent adverse federal laws should also be developed. If cooperative approaches to promote positive goals are developed, they might be used for defensive purposes as well. These might include efforts to prevent cutbacks in OEO programs for disadvantaged students, reduction of federal support of student financial aid, restrictions on NSF and other grant programs which have aided in professional development of faculties, lack of funding for building assistance programs, as well as restrictive or punitive laws governing federal aid to students.

The same cooperative mechanisms can be useful with respect to state legislation. The University's Office of the Dean of Administration could serve as an information source to the Coordinator's Office on matters of state bills and laws, with similar sources in the other colleges. Cooperative efforts may be worthwhile on such issues as loyalty oaths, special state study commissions on higher education in Massachusetts, and general state programs of financial aid to students.

RECOMMENDATION

The Coordinator should request an individual in one of the colleges to act as a resource person on legislative information, or should provide the service himself. This person should survey each institution to determine what bulletins, newsletters, and other materials are received dealing with state and federal legislation, and a procedure for exchange of information should be established. Each institution should tell the resource person who at that institution can provide him with current information in this area. He should maintain a current file on pertinent legislation. On his advice, the Coordinator should report and, if necessary, recommend action to the Presidents or other responsible college officials.

The Governance of Five-College Cooperation

THE GOVERNANCE OF five-college cooperation should preserve and enhance diversity among our institutions while encouraging development of those cooperative programs which will assist each institution to offer the best possible education to its students with the most rational and efficient use of its scarce resources. This requires the active involvement of all elements of the academic communities.

One of the problems with the cooperative decision-making process at present is that it has been too hidden from view and has, therefore, seemed to be more exclusive than it is in fact. Channels for bringing ideas and issues to the consideration of the community have been unclear. Lack of information and lack of clear lines of responsibility for formulating and carrying out policy have led to misunderstandings, frustrations, and some conflicts of purpose. The following paragraphs describe the situation.

The present system is relatively simple. The Five College Coordinator is responsible to the five Presidents for initiating or facilitating cooperation and seeing that agreed programs are carried out. The Presidents meet at least four times a year with the Coordinator to establish overall policy for cooperation, approve or disapprove proposed programs, and determine budgets. The Deputies of the Presidents meet with the Coordinator each month when there is no presidential meeting. Suggested programs are generally discussed by the Deputies and then decided upon by the Presidents.

This is only the visible part of the decision-making process. Much of the most important cooperative activity begins completely without reference to the Deputies, the Presidents, or even the Coordinator. Department heads get together to consider faculty appointments in the five-college context. Interinstitutional cooperation in the teaching of specific courses or advanced seminars often evolves from such meetings. Business officers agree among themselves on common approaches to problems. The Five College Student Coordinating Board began an evening bus service, which is now being continued as part of the comprehensive bus system to which the student governments contribute significant support. Faculty members with common interests gather for informal seminars, such as that in the Humanities.

In addition to the decision-making apparatus described above, there is a formal structure called Five Colleges, Incorporated. It was established in 1965 as Four Colleges, Incorporated, and with the admission of Hampshire College in 1966, it was given the present name. Its purpose is broadly defined so as to cover any and all possible cooperative arrangements. Its first formal function was to provide sponsorship for five-college charter flights to Europe. With the employment in the fall of 1967 of a full-time Coordinator not associated with any of the institutions, it was decided to use Five Colleges, Inc., as the channel for financial support of his office and of certain programs.

There is no formal five-college general deliberative body through which faculty or student views can be expressed. The Long Range Planning Committee this year is the nearest approximation to such a body we have had. The Five College Student Coordinating Board provides a forum for student discussion, but its role is not clearly delineated. There are no clear channels through which information about decisions involving cooperation can be disseminated within the several institutions. Trustees are not involved except to the degree to which the Presidents inform them. The same is true of alumni. No outside points of view are solicited in a formal or regular fashion.

A. Objectives

The LRPC believes that the governance of five-college cooperation should be founded upon the following principles:

1. More elements of the several academic communities should contribute to the making of policy—faculty, students, and administrative officers.
2. The five Presidents should continue to be the final decision-making authority on major programs.
3. There should be one senior person within each institution whose primary responsibilities are to see that possibilities for cooperation are considered in all major institutional decisions, to ensure that agreed cooperative arrangements are carried out, and to provide the Coordinator with a channel for obtaining institutional decisions or views on minor questions.
4. There should be interlocking membership between five-college groups and the committees within each institution dealing with similar subjects.
5. Channels should be developed for bringing issues to five-college consideration and for disseminating information about five-college activities within each institution. (For the latter purpose, the LRPC early recommended that the Coordinator begin a Five College Newsletter: Volume I, consisting of four issues, appeared during 1968–69.)
6. Any structure established should be sufficiently flexible to encourage individual contacts at all levels.

The Academic Policy Advisory Council

The establishment of the Academic Policy Advisory Council (APAC) is related to the first principle stated above, and its proposed functions and membership are discussed in Section I. The central importance of APAC in the thinking of the LRPC is illustrated by the number of recommendations in this report concerning subjects to be referred to it for further study. APAC will be concerned primarily with academic matters. It is proposed that the Deputies continue to meet regularly with the Coordinator as the overall coordinating group under the Presidents on all matters not within the purview of APAC. It is proposed further that the role of the Deputies within each institution be considerably strengthened and enlarged to enable them to fulfill the third objective listed above.

B. The Five College Deputies

AT PRESENT the Deputies, in theory and in fact, are Deputies only for the Presidents. There are no agreed criteria for appointment. The present Amherst Deputy is a faculty member who, as previous Coordinator, has much experience with cooperation. The Mount Holyoke Deputy is the Registrar. The Hampshire Deputy is the Dean of the School of Social Science. The Smith Deputy is the Assistant to the President, a faculty member appointed to that position for several years and given released time from most of his teaching to enable him to discharge his administrative functions. The University Deputy is the Assistant to the Provost. The LRPC believes the Deputies should continue to represent the Presidents but that they should also be given broader responsibilities. It is proposed that the Deputies be made responsible for the following:

1. Maintaining contact with people within their institutions who are involved in cooperative enterprises.
2. Providing advice for those with ideas for improving or expanding cooperation.
3. Informing people about cooperative plans or programs affecting them.
4. Developing and furnishing institutional views or decisions on proposed cooperative programs for the Coordinator.
5. Ensuring that five-college possibilities be considered at all levels of activity within the institutions.
6. Facilitating the implementation of agreed cooperative programs within the institution.
7. Serving on the Five College Academic Policy Advisory Council (APAC).
8. Constituting collectively the major policy advisory body on cooperative enterprises that do not fall within the jurisdiction of APAC to advise the Presidents and the Coordinator.
9. Recommending the structures, terms of reference, and memberships of five-college committees, including those recommended in this report, not otherwise provided for.
10. Keeping informed of all cooperative activities and discussions. (Hence, all five-college committees or groups which meet regularly should send copies of their minutes routinely to the Deputies and to the Coordinator.)
11. Continuing the work begun by the LRPC in consultation with all appropriate five-college groups, including the Five College Student Coordinating Board.

Many of these functions are now being performed by the Deputies to a limited extent. To improve the operation, the LRPC suggests that each President establish that the position of Five College Deputy is of major importance within each institution, appoint to the position a senior faculty or academic staff member who has the confidence of the President, faculty, and students, and release the Deputy from a major portion of his other duties and provide appropriate clerical support to enable him to perform his functions. The Committee suggests that the Deputy be appointed for no less than a three-year term.

The LRPC believes these to be minimal requirements. The increase in the tempo of cooperation proposed in this report will result in considerably more work for the Deputies than has existed in the past. They will not only have more extensive five-college business to attend to, but should also be deeply involved in the decision-making process within their institutions. For example, the Deputy should serve on or sit with his institutional long range planning committee and on the educational policies committee so that he could relate their deliberations to cooperative planning. He will also need to meet with other groups within his institution from time to time.

C. The Five College Coordinator

THE FIVE COLLEGE COORDINATOR is the chief executive officer of five-college cooperation and as such must be fully informed on cooperative activities and as knowledgeable as possible about the five institutions he serves. Accordingly, it is taken for granted that he will be an *ex officio* member of all five-college councils, committees, or other groups which meet regularly and that he may designate appropriate members of his staff to represent him from time to time.

The LRPC believes that it might be useful to five-college cooperation to obtain occasionally the points of view of Trustees, alumni and a few outsiders who could bring different perspectives to bear upon our enterprise. The way in which this might be done deserves further study.

D. Five Colleges, Incorporated

THE BOARD OF DIRECTORS of Five Colleges, Inc., consists of the eleven Members of the Corporation (the five Presidents, the five principal Business Officers, and the Five College Coordinator) plus additional Directors (presently four) elected by these Members. There is generally one meeting per year of this group, meeting first as "Members of the Corporation" and then as the "Board of Directors," principally to meet legal requirements for the continuation of the corporation.

The Long Range Planning Committee proposes that the By-Laws of Five Colleges, Inc., be amended to provide a Board which is consonant with the present decision-making process by reducing the number of Members of the Corporation from eleven to six (the five Presidents and the Coordinator). The revised By-Laws should leave open the possibility of expanding the Board in the future, but as long as the Members were the only Directors, the regular quarterly meetings of the Presidents with the Coordinator would be formal meetings of the Board of Directors. This would relate the legal structure of Five Colleges, Inc., to the *de facto* decision-making process without requiring premature decisions on the future structure of the Board of Directors.

RECOMMENDATIONS

1. **Each institution should establish the position of Five College Deputy, make clear his focal role in cooperation, and appoint to the position a senior faculty or academic staff member, to be**

released from a major portion of his other duties, for a term of at least three years.

2. Continued study should be given to means of obtaining counsel from Trustees, alumni, and selected people from outside the Valley.
3. The By-Laws of Five Colleges, Inc., should be amended to provide for only six Members (the five Presidents and the Coordinator) and the Board of Directors for the time being should be composed of only those members.

The Economic Consequences of Cooperation

A. Budget, Staff & Economics

BROADLY STATED, the purpose of five-college cooperation is to enhance the ability of the members to educate their students by offering the wealth of resources of diverse institutions while obtaining some of those economies of scale and of sharing scarce resources which cooperation makes possible. Each institution has more needs than it can satisfy alone. No one of our five institutions is so financially independent that it cannot gain from cooperative approaches to new problems.

Five-College Budgets: Order of Magnitude

Five-college budgets include only those items on which formal agreements have been made to share costs, and not the costs of all facilities and services in support of cooperative programs. Furthermore, they are for the most part cash budgets rather than total cost budgets. The five-college budget approved for fiscal year 1969–70 is over $450,000. Of this, approximately $200,000 is shared by the operating institutions on a more or less equal basis for the support of the Coordinator's Office, transportation, HILC, and other joint services and programs. The balance of about $250,000 covers principally the cost of operating radio station WFCR and of the Astronomy Department, to both of which the University gives much the largest share of support.

Services and facilities which have not been included in the formal five-college budget include a variety of functions performed by the individual institutions in support of five-college operations. Examples include operation of the five-college charter flights by Amherst, management of intercollege transportation by Smith, accounting support by Amherst, facility support of station WFCR and the *Massachusetts Review* by the University, provision of office space and utilities to the Coordinator by Hampshire College, salaries of the Deputies, released faculty time in support of the *Massachusetts Review,* and many other items. It is estimated that if these items were budgeted they would increase the budget by approximately one-half.

Allocation of Costs

Some cooperative academic associations are supported by dues or fees from members computed on the basis of student enrollment. Were we to use that formula, the University would contribute in the ratio of 16 to 2.4 for Smith, to 1.7 for Mount Holyoke, to 1.2 for Amherst. Since the largest institution, with its extensive resources, might appear to have least to gain from cooperation, this would be inequitable. Yet it would seem equally unfair to reverse the ratios on the assumption that the smallest institution has most to gain and thus should contribute most.

In most programs, the five colleges split the costs evenly. In others, as indicated in the paragraphs above on budgets, costs are unevenly allocated. In the case of the Five College Astronomy Department, for example, costs are distributed according to allocation of faculty salaries to "local" or to "five-college" teaching. No formula has yet been worked out for cost sharing for all cooperative programs. Freedom from formula, in fact, makes possible flexibility in the adoption of programs in which institutions may have varying degrees of involvement.

With respect to student course exchange among the private colleges, the institution from which the student comes pays the receiving institution $150 per semester course. Because of state regulations, the University neither pays nor receives money. This fee bears little or no relationship to the actual cost of adding a student to a course at the receiving institution. While initially it was related to the tuition rates at the three private colleges, this relationship has been invalidated by increases in tuition charges and by the change from five to four courses a semester as the usual load. For these reasons, it may become necessary to review the exchange course fee. There may be additional reason for review after 1970 when Hampshire College opens, since this will lead to a further increase in student exchange.

The Five College Coordinator & Staff

The Five College Coordinator facilitates and administers cooperative enterprises among the five institutions under the ultimate policy direction of the five Presidents. He prepares budgets. He attends meetings of the Presidents, Deputies, Secretaries, Registrars, Business Officers, Librarians, and of multitudinous five-college faculty and student committees. He encourages meetings of department heads and of individuals interested in area studies, faculty seminars, service programs, community relations, and other matters which concern the whole five-college community. He talks about five-college cooperation to alumni groups, individual institutions interested in cooperation, and other consortia. In addition, he attempts to raise funds to assist various five-college enterprises.

Until this fall, the Coordinator's full-time staff consisted of the Five College Fellow and a secretary. The Five College Fellow is a recent graduate of one of the institutions who works in the Coordinator's Office for one year as an intern performing a wide variety of tasks to assist the Coordinator. During 1968–69, an additional staff member was employed on a part-time basis to assist the Five College Long Range Planning Committee.

It is impossible for a staff of this size to administer all cooperative enterprises. Over the years, therefore, a system has developed whereby individuals within the several institutions have taken responsibility for various aspects of the cooperative enterprises as part of their regular institutional duties. This system has the advantage of involving a large number of individuals in the cooperative effort and of utilizing existing talent in the five institutions. It also reduces considerably the number of staff required in the Coordinator's office, thereby keeping apparent five-college costs down.

The system also has several weaknesses, however. Individuals in the five institutions who have primary responsibility to their respective institutions must accept the additional load of five-college assignments. It is more difficult for the Coordinator effectively to control the budgets involved in the cooperative activities, as he lacks direct authority over the individuals spending the funds. There is little doubt that the diffusion of labor involves a diffusion of authority and of responsibility. The Long Range Planning Committee believes that the Coordinator must have not only the responsibility but also the authority and staff to carry out agreed five-college projects.

Throughout this report will be found suggestions of additional services to be furnished by the Coordinator's Office. It will not be possible to determine all future staff requirements until the full impact of the recommendations has been determined and until there are decisions on the extent and speed of implementation. The LRPC did conclude, however, that a general assistant to the Coordinator is urgently required, to work primarily on academic programs. The primary responsibility of the assistant will be to provide staff services and information to the various five-college groups and committees which will be created as a result of the implementation of the LRPC's recommendations. He will also assist in the preparation of proposals to foundations and government agencies for funding of programs or activities which would not be available to individual institutions. The five Presidents approved this recommendation in May, 1969, and an assistant has since been appointed.

The LRPC also anticipates that at some time in the future certain joint business functions and services, such as the operational control and further development of the five-college transportation system, maintenance of five-college accounts and budgets, and the operation of five-college charter flights might be transferred to the Coordinator's Office. If this is to be accomplished, it will be necessary to appoint a business officer to the staff of the Coordinator. When the five colleges develop more definite plans for a cooperative approach to problems relating to community service programs and for cooperative recruitment and special programs for the disadvantaged, the addition of further staff to coordinate this area of related programs will be necessary.

The Committee also recommends an increase in funds for transportation in order to facilitate student course exchange and increased social and cultural activities. Additional funds are needed as well for more departmental seminars and colloquia as a mechanism to bring five-college faculties together. These are discussed more fully in other sections of this report.

Economics of Cooperation

The LRPC does not foresee that five-college cooperation will result in absolute savings, that is, an actual reduction in the budgets of participating institutions. The pressures of inflation and the demands for new courses, new programs, and increased college involvement in the social problems of the community simply make such an expectation unrealistic.

Given these pressures, however, it is probable that cooperation will permit the five colleges to meet the challenge at less cost per college than if each undertook the programs alone. Relative savings, therefore, can be anticipated. Examples of programs which have probably produced relative savings over the past years include the Five College Astronomy Department, HILC, and African-Asian Studies. Although these programs have added to the budgets of each institution, they have enriched the Valley's educational programs and have fulfilled a need which otherwise might have been met by each institution individually, either less adequately or at a greater cost.

There is inherent in a cooperative effort a certain degree of inflexibility of choice and commitment which, in some instances, can and will tend to result in cost to the individual institution which would otherwise not have been incurred. If joint programs are undertaken, each institution makes a commitment to the others which, in good faith, it has to maintain unless there are strong and compelling reasons for a withdrawal. If such a commitment to a cooperative effort is continued in spite of the fact that it would not have been undertaken or continued in terms of the institution's priorities, the net result is, indeed, an increase in cost. It is, therefore, essential that each institution determine carefully, in terms of its own objectives, the types and extent of commitment it wants and can undertake in cooperation with the other institutions.

Looking to the future, it is quite apparent that relative economies resulting from cooperation will depend to a large degree on institutional self-discipline. The time to effect savings in a new program or curriculum offering is before the program is started. It is essential that each institution consider a cooperative effort among all, or some, of the five institutions before embarking individually on new programs. Once institutional commitments are made for facilities and/or staff, the opportunity for an effective five-college effort is greatly lessened.

In addition to the relative savings discussed above, cooperation offers intangible benefits which cannot be measured with any degree of precision. The LRPC believes that five-college cooperation has helped the colleges to maintain a large number of applications and enrollments of highly qualified students because of the attraction of five-college programs and combined activities. It also helps to maintain excellence and reduces turnover of the faculty because of the attraction of a larger number of specialists in the five-college community.

RECOMMENDATION

The staff of the Five College Coordinator should be increased as additional programs are authorized or brought under the direct supervision of the Coordinator's Office.

B. Cooperation in Fund Raising

AMHERST, MOUNT HOLYOKE, SMITH, and Hampshire Colleges are and will be dependent for operating funds on tuition and fees, income from endowments, and annual gifts and grants from private sources. The University of Massachusetts depends primarily on an annual operating appropriation from the Massachusetts legislature. In addition, the operating colleges and the University have research support from various sources, predominantly federal in origin, which contributes to the educational program and is more or less self-supporting. The private colleges (except Hampshire) rely primarily on their alumni, parents of alumni, and parents of undergraduate students for annual gifts for operations.

Capital gifts, generally used for buildings or endowment, come to the private colleges primarily from alumni. Amherst and Smith have relied almost wholly on alumni to pay for buildings, and in recent years have seldom built or renovated a building for which the funds were not in hand, promised, or in view. Although they, too, seek capital gifts for buildings, Mount Holyoke and Hampshire have also taken federal loans to finance new construction. In addition, Hampshire and the University have been eligible for and have received federal grants for construction under a program in which their growth rate is a favored criterion.

The University, however, relies primarily on state appropriations for academic buildings, and on a state financing authority for self-liquidating facilities such as dormitories, dining halls, and student unions.

The Future of Support for Higher Education

It is not necessary here to review the voluminous current literature on the financing of higher education. A number of schemes have been proposed to resolve the large problems, but no one knows when and how solutions will be found. The most obvious partner for the colleges—both public and private—is the federal government, and a number of existing programs listed under the Higher Education Acts of 1963 and 1965 have been of great help in certain areas, primarily construction and student aid. Unfortunately, the inflexibility imposed by restrictive criteria, the widely fluctuating levels of support for existing programs, the many delays, and the annually decreasing levels of appropriations for higher education since 1966 have made it difficult to rely on the federal government's partnership. The general institutional support sought from the federal government has not been readily forthcoming. It is no wonder that colleges rely heavily on their alumni and constantly search for other sources outside the government.

Over the years, the philanthropic foundations have provided large sums for higher education. Recently, however, the problems of the cities have gained a greater share of the foundations' attention. Consequently, there has been a leveling off of the dollar amounts granted to higher education and a reduction of the funds for education as a percentage of the total funds granted. At the same time, the total expenditures and total needs of higher education are increasing at a very rapid rate. This divergence is illustrated in Table II.

It is not possible to predict whether the present decline in support of higher education by foundations will continue, will stabilize at the present level, or will be reversed. But it seems reasonable to assume that the decline will continue, because the urban problems now at the center of foundation concern are not to be easily or quickly resolved, and the rate of growth of foundation assets and income does not parallel the rate of growth of higher education. Therefore, to stabilize or increase gross support of higher education, the foundations would have to commit increasingly larger proportions of their available resources.

Thus, as with the federal government, the future of foundation support of higher education is not at all certain. Alternative sources must constantly be cultivated. For private colleges, these alternative sources are mainly gifts from alumni and other individuals, and bequests.

Five-College Cooperation in Fund Raising

The increased interest in cooperation in recent years, and particularly the founding of Hampshire College and Five Colleges, Inc., have raised questions about the relationships among the colleges when fund raising activities are considered. Among those questions are:

1. Are appeals for funds to the alumni of a college the exclusive privilege of that college or may appeals be made under some circumstances to alumni of one college by one or more of the others?
2. Should some foundation and government applications for funds be made on a cooperative basis?

TABLE II

*Relationship between foundation grants to higher education and costs of higher education in the U.S. 1965–68**

	1965	1966	1967	1968
Dollars spent in higher education	15.00	16.90	18.80	20.40
Dollars raised by higher education	1.22	1.23	1.27	NA
Dollars distributed by foundations	.32	.30	.29	NA
Per cent of foundation dollars granted	26.00	24.00	22.00	NA
Foundation dollars as per cent of total	2.00	1.80	1.50	NA

* Figures other than percentages are in billions of dollars. Sources: U.S. Office of Education; American Alumni Council. NA: Not Available.

3. Should information about donors, or prospective donors, be shared?
4. Should Five Colleges, Inc., appeal for funds directly for its support, or for support of projects shared by the member colleges?
5. Should a regular program to provide information to the alumni of the five colleges about cooperative activities be tried?

The answers to these and other related questions should be judged in terms of the greatest return in financial support to each of the five institutions, but it may not be possible, given the current relationships among the colleges, to test any assumptions about fund raising actions for the individual and collective good.

Appeals to Alumni

Historically, the individual colleges have conducted annual appeals to their alumni for funds for current operations. Because the University is largely financed by government, alumni financial support is not a central consideration. For the three private colleges these appeals have achieved outstanding results. They are generally organized by the alumni themselves, and operating costs are funded in part out of the annual return, giving the activity a substantial independence from the college administration or trustees. Nevertheless, the alumni and alumni fund organizations have worked closely and harmoniously with them. None of the colleges has sought support from the alumni of any of the other colleges.

In sum, the relationship between the alumni and the colleges is a close and fruitful one which the alumni enjoy and on which the colleges rely. It seems to the Long Range Planning Committee both unfair and unwise to suggest that any one of the colleges be asked to make available to any of the other colleges its alumni lists for an annual appeal for funds.

Less easy to resolve is the question of capital gifts. There have been many families with associations at two of the colleges, and it has been tacitly understood that only when this is true can more than one of the colleges cultivate the family or individual for capital support. Tradition was broken in 1965, however, when Harold F. Johnson, an Amherst alumnus, pledged six million dollars for the founding of Hampshire College.

Since Hampshire's founding there have been, from time to time, conversations with individual alumni of one of the other colleges about possible support of Hampshire. Such conversations have been undertaken only with the full knowledge and concurrence of the President of the college whose alumnus was involved.

From one point of view, it can be argued that increasingly the five colleges are being represented to their collective alumni and to the world as a cooperative enterprise. Insofar as alumni think about and take seriously the idea that the colleges must cooperate if they are to survive, the five colleges together might successfully appeal for funds where an appeal from an individual college would appear futile. From this point of view it could be argued that special five-college appeals should be mounted.

Examined solely from the perspective of the fund raiser, it might also be argued that the colleges are discriminating against each other to their mutual disadvantage. An Amherst alumnus is a fair target for every fund raising appeal in America except for those of Hampshire, Mount Holyoke, and Smith Colleges, and the University of Massachusetts. Few people make their charitable contributions solely to one enterprise. The intriguing question is whether or not an appeal from one of the other colleges, in addition to Amherst, might or might not result in maintenance of the gift size to Amherst *and* a total increase in gifts to the Valley colleges.

On the other side of the argument is the high degree of dependence by the various colleges on their alumni for capital as well as annual gifts and the long-established proprietary feeling of the colleges for their alumni. The cooperative relationships among the colleges could be the first casualties in a fund raising free-for-all. It would be deleterious to the financial wellbeing of any one of the colleges to have major capital gifts diverted to one of the others, and it would be folly for any one of the colleges to risk the complex and delicate cooperative relationship for the sake of possible capital support from alumni of the other institutions.

In conclusion, it seems to the LRPC that the dependence of the colleges on their alumni for capital support, the current scarcity of capital funds, and the importance of the developing cooperative relationship argue strongly for a continuation of the present practice regarding solicitation of capital gifts by one college from alumni of another college.

Foundation and Government Applications

To date, the history of the application of the various colleges and the University to government sources or private philanthropic foundations for support has been similar to that of efforts to raise funds from alumni. That is, requests have been conducted with little regard to the possibility that a joint application requesting funding for a shared or cooperative effort among two or more of the colleges would be more successful than an application for a program at one institution. The Sloan Foundation program for undergraduate science support is an instance where cooperation rather than competition might have been advantageous to the colleges. Three of the four private colleges have received, within the past two years, grants under the Sloan Foundation program. (The program was for privately supported undergraduate colleges, so the University was not eligible.) It is conceivable, under the terms of the program, that the four colleges, had they coordinated and integrated their applications, might have received more money; and by working together they might have had an opportunity to lead the country in improvements in undergraduate science education which the three colleges working separately are unlikely to have. If such a thought crossed the minds of the science faculties or administrations of the colleges, no one entertained the idea seriously enough to try to arouse interest in it on his own or other campuses.

A number of other foundations have expressed an interest in the possibility of supporting cooperative programs as a possible demonstration of one way to increase effectiveness. The three grants of the Ford Foundation, the first of which resulted in the 1956 *Report of the Committee on Cooperation,* the second in the 1958 *New College Plan* (from which grew the initial idea of Hampshire College), and the substantial grant to promote cooperative development of an Asian-African program are notable. Included also must be the U. S. Steel Foundation grant of five thousand dollars in 1968 and the Richard King Mellon Trust grant in March, 1969, of one hundred thousand dollars to support the studies of the Long Range Planning Committee and their implementation. A more recent gift of ten thousand dollars from the Gulf Oil Corporation for geology equipment to be used cooperatively is another example.

The United States Office of Education has recognized the need for enlarging experimentation in cooperation and has instituted several programs, the objectives of which coincide, or could coincide, with ideas of current interest at two or more of the colleges. Examples are programs in support of shared computers, and for cooperative development of libraries. A newly authorized federal program called "Networks for Knowledge" is explicitly designed to promote a variety of cooperative arrangements.

In conclusion, the Committee believes that unrealized opportunities exist for the funding of cooperative programs by private foundations and the United States government, and that increased efforts should be made to cooperate in joint applications for such funding.

Sharing Information About Donors

In the areas of corporate, foundation, and government support, there is a high coincidence of effort among the colleges in gathering information, most of which is publicly (although not necessarily easily) available. The information is essential to the preparation of applications which are relevant to the interests of the funding agency and appropriate in other respects to the kind of support available.

It is important to distinguish between information gathering and application for funds. The former is relatively time consuming, is continuous in demand, requires meticulous care, and is essentially noncompetitive in nature. The latter may be competitive and certainly is time consuming, as well as requiring imaginatively and coherently written presentation.

During 1967, Amherst, Hampshire, and Mount Holyoke shared the cost of a government information officer appointed to Five Colleges, Inc., whose function was to gather information on federal programs of possible import and interest to one or more of the colleges, and to assist in the preparation and submission of applications for support. Although that experiment was not very fruitful, the participants agreed that its failure should not discourage attempts to find a more workable plan for such cooperation.

Since 1967, Amherst and Hampshire have shared the services and costs of a part-time foundations research assistant in New York who works primarily at the Foundation Library Center preparing informational reports on foundations of interest to either or both of the colleges. This arrangement is regarded as useful and the two institutions plan to continue it.

The Committee believes that efforts should be made to find ways to increase sharing of information about corporation, foundation, and government donors, with the objective of increasing the information available to all the colleges participating. It is recommended that consideration be given to expanding the shared information service to a full-time person shared by at least three of the institutions and employed to do research in corporate as well as foundation giving.

Each of the colleges already has a substantial library of information about corporate, foundation, and government sources. It would be a relatively easy matter for each development office to index its library and to make a small card catalogue which could be used on the premises by the other colleges as an index to information to be shared. To assist in the exchange and sharing of information, one person could be designated at each office to be responsible for this function. Costs of joint efforts should be shared.

Five Colleges, Incorporated, Funding

People in the government and foundations who believe that cooperation among colleges is one way to strengthen higher education are especially interested in the five-college cooperative relationship because it includes both public and private institutions, because of the effects that cooperation among institutions with high prestige could have on education elsewhere, and because of interest in the creation of a new college as a product of cooperation.

There is some evidence from the funding support already received that foundations and government officials are ready to assist the colleges to make a serious effort at expanded cooperation. The Mellon Trust grant is the best, although not the only, example of such interest. The report of the Five College Long Range Planning Committee is likely to call attention to, and increase interest in, the five colleges and their plans, and will provide an opportune time for a funding effort to begin. The LRPC believes, therefore, that Five Colleges, Inc., should begin to campaign in earnest during fiscal year 1969–70 for funds to supplement contributions from the colleges in support of cooperative activities.

A definition is needed of activities for which funds are to be sought, and there should be a statement of goals, a timetable, and an estimate of staffing needs. Although the Coordinator will lead the effort, with assistance from the Presidents and Development Officers of the colleges, it is likely that an additional person will be needed to assist the Coordinator in raising funds as more cooperative projects are developed and as the fruitfulness of fund-raising efforts is demonstrated. The LRPC recommends that the Coordinator prepare plans for a fund-raising effort in behalf of Five Colleges, Inc., for review and approval by the Presidents.

Information Program

The cooperation between Amherst, Mount Holyoke, Smith, and the University has been attractive to the alumni, perhaps because some believed that the financial pressures upon the private colleges could be lessened through a sharing of certain scarce resources or expensive programs. The founding of Hampshire, based on assumptions about the value of cooperation at a time when the colleges' financial problems are becoming more severe, has heightened interest in cooperation. In addition, Hampshire seems to have a special fascination to many alumni who regard it with pride as a logical and bold effort by their own alma maters to help resolve higher education's problems.

Continuing the interest and support of the alumni of any college is going to depend increasingly on the ability of the college to respond successfully to changes generated within the institution or imposed from without by a changing society and the effectiveness of the communication of these responses to persons interested in the college. The Committee believes that information about cooperative activities should be reported on a regular basis through the alumni magazines. It would be preferable to have the same article or story appear in all magazines for the sake of efficiency and consistency. This has been successfully done twice so far: in 1967 all magazines carried an insert on "Five College Cooperation," and in 1968 three carried an article on "Music in the Valley." The Committee hopes this can continue on an annual basis, one of the four editors perhaps taking responsibility for the cooperative section for the year.

RECOMMENDATIONS

1. **The relationships between the colleges and their respective alumni should be respected, and the present policies regarding the solicitation of capital gifts by one college from the alumni of another college should be continued.**
2. **The Development Officers should establish means for increasing efforts to make joint application to foundations and the federal government for the funding of cooperative programs.**
3. **Consideration should be given by the Development Officers to the possibility of sharing the expense of a full-time person in some central location, probably New York, to do research on prospective foundation and corporate support sources.**
4. **Information at each of the colleges about corporate, foundation, and government sources of support should be made available to the other colleges on a basis to be established by the Development Officers.**
5. **The Coordinator should establish a statement of goals and a timetable for funding Five Colleges, Inc., activities, and should begin a campaign for funds.**
6. **The colleges should begin an information program about five-college cooperation. Some news should appear in each issue of each alumni magazine, and there should be a common insert on a major subject once a year.**

Conclusion: The Priorities

When the Long Range Planning Committee began its consideration of the direction five-college cooperation should take in the future, it had a wide range of choices. At one extreme it might have recommended movement toward merger, or at the other extreme return to separatism. Neither of these extremes was thought to be worth long discussion.

A third possibility was to recommend that the five colleges continue cooperating much as they do now. As the LRPC considered the present state of cooperation, however, it soon decided that this also was an unsatisfactory position. There is little doubt that cooperation as it now exists benefits all the institutions, but there is also little doubt that it could be improved. The recommending and decision-making process is haphazard and unclear. Important members of the college communities not only are ill-informed about what is happening, but have little or no part in establishing policy. Cooperative projects are ad hoc and peripheral to the main purposes of the several institutions, initiated not through conscious planning, but as a result of individual initiative. Priorities are often determined not as a result of thoughtful consideration of the character and purposes of the institutions, but by choosing among individual projects on the basis of their relative short-term attractiveness. The rationale for cooperative services is not clearly defined. In sum, the LRPC concluded that despite considerable progress to date, the five institutions have not yet approached the best use of cooperation to help solve some of the serious problems they all face.

The Committee realizes that one of the great strengths of American higher education in general, and of the five Valley institutions in particular, lies in diversity. No one institution can or should try to have all the resources to meet all the educational needs of all students. The Committee recognized at an early stage that it would be impossible to maintain diversity unless means were found to utilize available educational resources more efficiently. It decided that one of the most promising means for maintaining and enhancing diversity among the five colleges lies in enlarging cooperation. The very fact of that cooperation, indeed, gives to the five colleges one of their most distinctive features within the world of higher education; it is itself an increasingly significant part of the identity of each institution.

The many recommendations contained in this report range from suggestions that certain matters need further study to proposals of detailed steps which could be taken at once. Some recommendations are of major importance and some propose only minor changes in procedure. A few urgent recommendations were carried out while the report was in preparation; others may take years to accomplish. The LRPC therefore decided to conclude its report with a reiteration of its views on the critical issues involved in cooperation and an indication of those recommendations which it believes to be of highest priority.

The essential point of this report is that the five institutions should move deliberately and thoughtfully toward greater academic complementarity. Cooperative possibilities should thus be consciously and explicitly considered in arriving at all major institutional decisions. Each proposed faculty appointment, either to fill a vacancy or to staff a new position, every new academic program, and every proposed new building or major equipment purchase should be justified in the five-college context within the institution. Any institution would remain free, of course, to make an appointment or construct a building which appears to duplicate other resources, but should explicitly consider its possible relationship to five-college cooperation before doing so.

So that all may be aware of cooperative possibilities, the five institutions should establish councils or committees in those key areas in which they agree that the advantages of cooperation are most important. When there exist recommendations from such a five-college council or committee, an institution which makes an appointment or decides upon the addition of a major academic program or facility contrary to these recommendations should state clearly to the other institutions and to the Five College Coordinator that it is doing so and why.

Institutional self-control requires discipline. It is taken for granted within each institution that a given faculty appointment, new academic program, or new building must be viewed in its relationship to the whole. A faculty committee, the Dean, or the President will impose internal discipline in this sense.

There is no means for imposing external discipline upon the individual institutions, nor does any member of the LRPC believe that anything resembling a five-college government to provide such external discipline should be established. Rather, the Committee suggests means for better exchange of information, improved cooperative planning, enhancing the climate for cooperation, and obtaining a more considered, continuous, and disciplined approach to cooperation within each institution. The Committee has also recommended several possible new cooperative programs. Of the many subjects considered, the Committee recommends that the institutions give first attention to nine.

1. Greatly strengthen and enlarge the role of the Five College Deputies (Section X). Our mutual interest requires within each institution one person responsible both for ensuring that cooperative possibilities are considered within the institution and for representing the institution in the principal policy-recommending bodies under the Presidents.

The LRPC recommends that each President appoint to the position of Deputy a senior member of the faculty or academic staff who enjoys the confidence of the administration, the faculty, and the students, release him from a major part of his other duties, and provide him with clerical help.

2. **Create a Five College Academic Policy Advisory Council** (Section I). This body should include from each institution the Deputy, a faculty member from the committee on educational policy, and a student. With the Coordinator, this would be a sixteen-member council which would have the responsibility to consider proposals from interdisciplinary studies councils and from faculty and student committees, to initiate its own proposals, and to advise both the Presidents and the faculties on academic policy issues that affect five-college cooperation.

3. **Establish certain five-college geographic area councils and other interdisciplinary studies councils** as an additional means for obtaining responsible consideration of cooperative academic programs (Section II). Five-college interdisciplinary committees which have considered academic programs in the past have depended for their effectiveness so greatly on individual initiative that faculty leaves or moves have often disrupted the continuity of committee work. Furthermore, there has been no recognized means for relating the work of the committee to other cooperative programs. To make possible effective working relationships, the LRPC believes that the area and interdisciplinary councils should report to the Five College Academic Policy Advisory Council.

Among the proposed interdisciplinary studies councils, the Committee sees the establishment of those proposed for Black Studies and for Urban Studies as the most urgent. These areas of study are relatively new additions to the curriculum of all the colleges. Both attract great student interest. Both are areas in which there are limited numbers of qualified teachers. Competition among the colleges in establishing these programs would be destructive of the quality of all of them.

4. **Establish a Field Office for Urban and Regional Studies** (Section V.B). The Presidents of the colleges have already approved the proposal from the committee established to study the idea, and a search for funds is under way. The Field Office is much needed for enriching the academic offerings in Urban and Environmental Studies. It relates to the proposed creation of an Urban Studies Council.

5. **Establish a Five College Committee for Educational Opportunity** (Section V.A). All the colleges have adopted programs for increased recruitment of and assistance to disadvantaged students. There is no need for the institutions to have identical programs, but there is great need for them to share information and resources so that each can offer the best program possible.

6. **Enlarge the opportunities for student course exchange** (Section III). A major benefit of five-college cooperation is the opportunity it gives students to take courses at more than one institution. The LRPC recommends the adoption of a new criterion to govern course exchange. The catalogue language proposed is that a qualified student, with the consent of his adviser, may take a course on another campus "if the course is significantly different from any available to him on his own campus." The Committee also thinks it is important for each institution to set up a process by which the student and his adviser may gain more information about proposed exchange courses and by which disagreements about them may be resolved.

7. **Improve the transportation system,** because of its importance to student course exchange and to other cooperative programs (Section VIII.B).

8. **Adopt the Four-One-Four calendar in all five institutions** (Section IV). The LRPC is convinced that such a calendar is academically sound, that it will facilitate course exchange among the colleges, and that the five cooperating

institutions can provide special opportunities for a January term which will offer new and valuable educational experiences for both students and faculty members.

9. **Take the initiative, in cooperation with their communities, in the establishment of Committees for a Better Local Environment in each of the towns** (Section IX.A). The colleges would participate with other groups in these Committees and offer to them technical advice and information when needed.

The LRPC is aware that the implementation of several of its recommendations will require the most careful consideration. It is also clear that acceptance of some of them will result in the need for additional five-college staff. Money will be required for other purposes as well, and provisions must be made for more extensive exchange of information, including such items as faculty inventories and catalogue listings of courses at all institutions.

The Committee is unanimous, however, in believing that the benefits which can accrue to all of the institutions from carrying out the recommendations listed in this report will far outweigh anticipated costs.

Summary of Recommendations

I. Academic Complementarity

1. Improvement in the system of faculty exchange among the five colleges should be a subject for continuing study by departments and by the Five College Academic Policy Advisory Council. Released-time borrowing rather than overtime borrowing should be encouraged. The possibility of offering graduate teaching as a part of the regular duties of some college faculty members should be explored by the University and any of the colleges that would like such an option.

2. Exchange of information among the five colleges should be substantially increased. An inventory of faculty resources should be developed and published on an annual basis. A means should be found for making more readily available to all students and faculty members in the Valley information on the course offerings of all the institutions.

3. Each of the five institutions should accept the principle, and find means for ensuring, that any proposal for a new course, instructional program, or major facility include a statement setting forth the relationship between it and the offerings of the other institutions, with explicit discussion of the possibilities of five-college cooperation and the reasons for proceeding either cooperatively or unilaterally.

4. If one institution decides not to act in accordance with the advice or recommendations of an official five-college

committee, the President should, in writing, inform the other institutions and the Coordinator of the decision and of the reasons for it.

5. A Five College Academic Policy Advisory Council (APAC) should be established, to include from each institution a faculty member representing the chief educational policy committee, a student chosen from the senior academic committee on which students serve, and the five-college Deputy. All five-college academic committees and councils should report to APAC.

II. Cooperative Academic Programs & Activities

1. Geographic Area Councils, constituted of faculty and student representatives of each of the five institutions, should be established for the areas of the Soviet Union and Eastern Europe, Latin America, East Asia, South and Southeast Asia, and the Middle East. These Councils should take as their explicit aim the achievement of complementary resources in faculty, library, and curriculum among the five colleges.

2. A Black Studies Council composed of faculty and student representatives of each institution should be established to advance the creation and coordination of Black Studies courses and programs.

3. A five-college faculty-student Urban Studies Council should be established, with responsibility for investigating the possibilities for coordinated development of courses and programs.

4. Two Arts Councils should be established, one for the Fine Arts (drawing, painting, sculpture, ceramics, architecture, and other visual and plastic arts), and another for Performing Arts (music, dance, and dramatic arts). They should have both student and faculty representatives from each institution. Among the subjects the two Councils should consider are increased exchange of information concerning courses, faculty, and programs; coordination of course sched-

uling; faculty exchange and complementary hiring; coordination of events and exhibitions, and publication of a common calendar; cooperation in the use of facilities, materials, and libraries; a five-college summer program in the arts; and the proposal for a five-college Center for Experimental Media.

5. A five-college faculty-student Film Council should be established to coordinate the colleges' film library acquisitions and the use of films from the University Film Study Center. It should explore the wide range of possibilities for complementary development of film courses, materials, spaces, and faculty. The present college representatives on the Center Committee might appropriately be made members of the Council.

6. Department heads and other administrators should actively encourage the formation or continuation of cooperative colloquia and faculty seminars.

7. Under policies established by the Academic Policy Advisory Council, financial support should be provided for up to ten faculty seminars at $300–$500 each per year.

8. The participants in faculty seminars should consider the desirability of organizing councils similar to the proposed Area Studies Councils for purposes of disseminating information and promoting the appointment of complementary faculty specialists and the development of complementary library resources and courses of study.

9. A five-college committee should be appointed to explore the possibility of cooperation in overseas study activities and to prepare recommendations for instituting and sustaining such cooperation. It should establish a mechanism for exchanging information on overseas study programs.

10. The Academic Policy Advisory Council should discuss the Five College Astronomy Department and assist in resolving any conflict there may be between its undergraduate and graduate interests.

11. The Academic Policy Advisory Council should consider whether, and under what conditions, the joint depart-

ment provides a suitable structure for coordinating course offerings in other fields of study.

12. The Academic Policy Advisory Council should consider the circumstances in which joint appointments are useful and should establish guidelines for administering such appointments. It should also consider instituting a program of Five College Visiting Scholars.

13. The present History of Science Committee should continue its coordination of recruitment of faculty in that field.

14. The Academic Policy Advisory Council should consider increased cooperation in graduate programs with a view to devising a more systematic method for bringing faculty members at the private colleges into direct contact with the University's graduate program, either by direct participation in the program or by finding opportunities to employ University graduate students in the educational activities of the colleges. It should recommend ways of attaining maximum advantage from the cooperative Ph.D. program and should explore the possibilities for improved cooperation in M.A.T. programs designed for potential community college teachers as well as for secondary school teachers.

III. Student Course Exchange

1. In addition to recognizing the merits of exchange courses in specialized fields within a student's major which are not available on his own campus and of courses in an appropriate discipline which may not be represented at all on the home campus, the five colleges should recognize the value of an exchange course which offers a significantly different educational experience to the student even in a subject which overlaps a course available on the home campus. Where a proposed exchange course makes reasonable academic sense for a student's program, the five colleges

should also recognize the merit for a student's educational development of gaining some experience of a different educational atmosphere.

2. The existing catalogue statement governing the policy for course exchanges should substitute the phrase "if the course is significantly different from any available to him on his own campus" for the present wording, which says "if the course is not available to him on his own campus."

3. Each institution should establish some process by which a student and his adviser can gain further information on a proposed exchange course. The student should be allowed to present his case to higher authority if this information-gathering process does not resolve a disagreement.

4. Greater efforts should be made to make available information on courses at all the institutions in the form of syllabi, reading lists, and course critiques.

5. Preregistration for exchange courses should be conducted in a specified period before regular registration periods at the five colleges, or the period for dropping and adding courses should be extended.

6. Departments at the five colleges should be encouraged to share information on their courses and establish procedures for advising and admitting exchange students.

7. There should be a continuing effort among the five colleges to make as nearly simultaneous as possible the opening and closing of the academic year, the examination periods which close each term, the advising and registration periods, and the time of appearance of course catalogues.

8. Five-college guidelines should be established to govern the setting of quotas for exchange students in classes likely to be oversubscribed.

IV. The Four-One-Four Calendar

1. The five institutions should adopt a common Four-One-Four calendar (four months—one month—four months) and

plan for a January term to include forms of educational experience not ordinarily available as well as forms of five-college cooperation not now possible.

2. This common calendar should be adopted after the Five College Academic Policy Advisory Council has investigated the experience and the plans of other consortia concerning cooperative plans for an interim term and submitted to the five faculties for action a full report proposing a cooperative plan for programs appropriate to the five colleges during a January term.

V. Supplementary Academic Activities

1. A new Committee for Educational Opportunity should be appointed to replace the present Five-College Committee on Social Responsibility. Its membership should include faculty members, administrators, and students from the five colleges who are qualified by position and experience to carry out the functions listed below.

2. This committee should serve as a clearinghouse for information about programs for the disadvantaged on all five campuses; it should be consulted prior to the establishment of individual institutional programs; and it should consider, evaluate, and propose, where appropriate, joint programs:

- for assisting admissions officers in the recruitment of disadvantaged students with the express purpose of increasing the number reached;
- for defining admission criteria for high-risk students;
- for developing a five-college summer program to facilitate subsequent matriculation of more high-risk students than the three private colleges are currently admitting;
- for soliciting funds, in cooperation with institutional development officers, to finance programs developed and to provide supplementary financial aid for increased numbers of disadvantaged students enrolled;

- for developing four- or five-college tutorial and counseling services to assist institutions to recognize and provide for the needs of their disadvantaged students (a coordinator-trainer might be jointly financed by four or five colleges to give advice and provide training for those involved in the individual campus programs);
- for proposing and developing programs to assist the white members of the five-college communities to recognize and act upon attitudes and practices which require change.

3. Because the implementation of the above recommendations requires some Committee staff services in addition to the coordinator-trainer mentioned above, additional staff should be provided to the Five College Coordinator.

4. High priority should be given to obtaining the funds with which to establish a Field Office for Urban and Regional Studies.

5. A committee should be appointed to study and report to the institutions on the possibilities of cooperative summer programs. It should establish a clearinghouse for information about summer programs and events on individual campuses.

6. A five-college committee should be established to consider joint action in continuing education, including recommendations of necessary steps for implementation.

7. The alumni directors should jointly study and report on the possible establishment of cooperative programs of continuing education for alumni either held on campus in connection with reunions or summer programs or established in selected places around the country.

VI. Coeducation & Cooperation

1. All five institutions should recognize that one of the purposes of cooperation is to assist the single-sex colleges

to provide for their students some of the advantages of coeducation.

2. Consultation and the sharing of information on the subject of coeducation should be continued as a matter of routine among the five institutions. The Presidents of Amherst, Mount Holyoke and Smith should agree that no one of them will make decisions on or take major steps toward coeducation without prior consultation with the other Presidents. Consideration should be given by all five institutions to ways in which they might assist each other to maintain or to introduce the patterns chosen by each.

VII. Student Life

1. The Deans of Students of the five institutions should meet regularly with student representatives to consider ways of increasing student movement among the institutions and encouraging joint activities.

2. A five-college program of education about drugs should be initiated and the health services should make a joint study of the subject.

3. The rules for student conduct on each campus and the disciplinary action that may be expected in case of violation should be made known to all students in the Valley. An attempt should also be made to have rules and disciplinary procedures as closely aligned as possible. When there is an infraction, a judiciary representative from the campus where the violation occurred should sit in as adviser to the violator's home judiciary.

4. A single individual at each institution should be designated to be the source of information about student housing and to work with his counterparts at the other institutions and with student representatives toward the development of a joint code for off-campus student housing consonant with existing local codes.

5. The five institutions should encourage public and private initiative in the development of recreational programs and facilities likely to benefit students.

VIII. Cooperative Planning and Use of Facilities & Services

1. The Physical Facilities Inventory of each institution being completed for the State Higher Education Facilities Commission should be placed on file in the Coordinator's Office.

2. Twice annually, in January and July, the planning officers of each institution should submit to the Coordinator's Office for circulation to all other planning officers a report of projects in construction and of pending or planned projects, including, when possible, building programs.

3. Each institution should make its building plans available to the Coordinator on his request, and at the expense of his office.

4. Those responsible for physical facilities planning should meet at least four times a year to discuss areas of common interest.

5. The colleges should recognize that improved transportation is essential to academic cooperation and that substantial annual expenditures upon it are to be anticipated.

6. Funds should be sought to bring in a consultant or consultants to make a study of our transportation needs and to recommend ways to meet them, including consideration of a five-college motor pool to buy, service, and dispatch all vehicles, including five-college buses; and the possibilities of a student-run bus system.

7. The Five College Computer Committee and its three subcommittees on academic, administrative, and library uses of computers should continue to coordinate computer planning in the Valley through the exchange of information on institutional needs and plans. The committee should pro-

pose formal cooperative arrangements when appropriate and should encourage the fullest possible sharing of institutional computational facilities.

8. The four colleges should establish two systems design staffs, one for administrative and the other for library computer uses, to work with the appropriate University groups.

9. The standing computer committee should establish a means of circulating lists and abstracts of computer programs available in the Valley which are likely to be of use to others in the five-college area.

10. The Academic Policy Advisory Council should establish the priority to be assigned to obtaining a thorough study of the potential academic uses of electronic instruments to support teaching.

11. If the Council considers the above subject to be of high priority, a study should be launched with internal resources, by the Audio-Visual Center at the University, for example, or funds should be sought to employ a consulting firm.

12. The Hampshire Inter-Library Center should be continued as an independent library. The Board of Directors should continue its study of ways in which the Center's budget might be increased and dues be assessed more equitably. The Board should also review functions which might be added to those now performed by HILC should additional funds be provided.

13. The Librarians of the five colleges should consider instituting a fee and/or pass system whereby each library would grant in-person borrowing and building use privileges to a limited number of faculty and students from the other four institutions.

14. The Librarians of the five colleges should be supported in their project of expanding the union list of serials now in preparation so that it will provide complete serial holdings information in book form. It should be issued on an annual basis.

15. The four private colleges should form a library sys-

tems and procedures group to work with that of the University library in designing compatible library computer applications.

16. Existing museum collections should be inventoried, and their contents should be classified in two categories: those objects that an institution wishes to store on its own campus for exhibition and study there, and those objects which, although of sufficient interest to rule out sale or discard, the owning institution would be willing to have placed under five-college operation and housed elsewhere than on its home campus.

17. The directors of collections which institutions wish to continue on their home campuses should meet to discuss the possible value of such cooperative activities as a union catalogue of the collections, making portions of one collection available on loan at one of the other campuses, joint sponsorship of loan exhibitions brought in from outside the Valley, and synchronization of plans for loan exhibitions on individual campuses. The possibility that acquisition programs might involve exchanges of information and joint planning should also be explored. If, as the collections grow, policies could be developed on the extent to which individual institutions should specialize their collections, the usefulness and interest of the combined collections would be enhanced.

18. If there are collections of significance which the individual institutions prefer not to maintain and exhibit on their own, the possibility of joint exhibitions should be explored. It might prove desirable to invite representatives of the community to explore with the colleges the establishment of a Valley Museum Foundation, which would ultimately be responsible for the operation of a Valley museum or museums in which some of the collections of the five institutions might be housed.

19. A committee should be appointed to determine the best arrangement for increased intensive care services for mental health and to submit a report on the feasibility of

establishing a five-college halfway house to serve students for whom continued academic work is judged possible despite psychiatric disability.

20. One five-college representative should be appointed to explore the feasibility of five-college participation in the future efforts of the community mental health organization for the area.

21. A five-college committee should be appointed to recommend, in consultation with Deans of Students and with students, ways to foster human development programs, particularly cooperative programs for education on sex and drugs.

22. The Coordinator's office should prepare a brochure on five-college cooperation for the use of admissions offices.

23. The Directors of Admissions should prepare a report on the possibility of increased cooperation in recruiting.

24. Consideration should be given to putting colloquia for guidance counselors on a four- or five-college basis.

25. Hampshire College's offer of land for a Five College Center should be formally accepted by Five Colleges, Inc., and the site should be determined.

26. A planning committee should be established to determine the functions and costs of a Five College Center and to make a formal proposal to the Presidents for its establishment and funding.

IX. Community Relations & Public Service

1. The five colleges should take the initiative in forming, in cooperation with their communities, Committees for a Better Local Environment in their respective towns, with broad representative membership.

2. One person from each institution who is serving on the committee for his area should also be designated as representative on a Five-College Local Environment Committee which would help serve the local committees by providing

information about special resources available within the five colleges, and which would coordinate the participation of the five colleges in environmental development.

3. The five colleges should encourage faculty and staff members to participate as individual citizens in official and unofficial groups concerned with the preservation and development of the environment.

4. The five colleges should work with responsible citizens' groups which are trying to increase the availability of low- and moderate-cost housing.

5. Before liberalizing existing regulations, the colleges should study the availability of housing and the environmental consequences of permitting large numbers of students to live in non-college housing.

6. The colleges should consider developing minimum standards for off-campus student housing and requiring all units to be placed on an approved list prior to rental to students.

7. An inventory of community services should be compiled and maintained under the auspices of the Five College Coordinator.

8. Students or faculty from one institution should be able to participate in service programs of another institution whenever feasible.

9. Both the Coordinator's Office and the Field Office for Urban and Regional Studies should be able to give information to members of the community about the services available from the colleges.

10. The Coordinator should request an individual in one of the colleges to act as a five-college resource person on legislative information or should provide the service himself. This person should survey each institution to determine what bulletins, newsletters, and other materials are received dealing with state and federal legislation, and a procedure for exchange of information should be established. Each institution should tell the resource person who in that institution can provide him with current information in this

area. He should maintain a current file on pertinent legislation. On his advice, the Coordinator should report and, if necessary, recommend action to the Presidents or other responsible college officials.

X. The Governance of Five-College Cooperation

1. Each institution should establish the position of Five College Deputy, make clear his focal role in cooperation, and appoint to the position a senior faculty or academic staff member, to be released from a major portion of his other duties, for a term of at least three years.

2. Continued study should be given to means of obtaining counsel from Trustees, alumni, and selected people from outside the Valley.

3. The By-Laws of Five Colleges, Inc., should be amended to provide for only six Members (the five Presidents and the Coordinator) and the Board of Directors for the time being should be composed of only those members.

XI. The Economic Consequences of Cooperation

1. The staff of the Five College Coordinator should be increased as additional programs are authorized or brought under the direct supervision of the Coordinator's Office.

2. The relationships between the colleges and their respective alumni should be respected, and the present policies regarding the solicitation of capital gifts by one college from the alumni of another college should be continued.

3. The Development Officers should establish means for increasing efforts to make joint application to foundations and the federal government for the funding of cooperative programs.

4. Consideration should be given by the Development Officers to the possibility of sharing the expense of a full-time person in some central location, probably New York, to do research on prospective foundation and corporate support sources.

5. Information at each of the colleges about corporate, foundation, and government sources of support should be made available to the other colleges on a basis to be established by the Development Officers.

6. The Coordinator should establish a statement of goals and a timetable for funding Five Colleges, Incorporated, activities, and should begin a campaign for funds.

7. The colleges should begin an information program about five-college cooperation. Some news should appear in each issue of each alumni magazine, and there should be a common insert on a major subject once a year.

Committees and Staff

A. Members of the Five College Long Range Planning Committee

Amherst College

Prosser Gifford, *Dean of the Faculty*
Theodore P. Greene, *Professor of History*
Kurt M. Hertzfeld, *Treasurer*

Hampshire College

Robert C. Birney, *Dean of School of Social Science*
Charles R. Longsworth, *Vice President*
Richard C. Lyon, *Dean of the College*

Mount Holyoke College

Lawrence E. Remillard, *Comptroller*
John L. Teall, *Professor of History*
Mary E. Tuttle, *Secretary of the College*

Smith College

Robert L. Ellis, *Treasurer*
Charles Henderson, Jr., *Professor of Classics*
George F. Mair, *Assistant to the President and Professor of Economics*

University of Massachusetts

David M. Clay, *Director of University Libraries* (served on LRPC after September, 1968)
William C. Havard, Jr., *Professor of Government*
Edward C. Moore, *Dean of the Graduate School* (served on LRPC in June and July, 1968)
Leo F. Redfern, *Dean of Administration* (As of August 1, 1969, President, Keene State College, N. H.)

Five College Coordinator

North Burn *(Chairman)*

B. Staff

Barbara Turlington, *Assistant to the LRPC*
Nora Fornas, *Secretary to the Five College Coordinator* (through May, 1969)
Barbara Moore, *Secretary to the Five College Coordinator* (from June, 1969)
Merilee Neunder, *Five College Fellow*

C. Committees established by the LRPC

1. PLANNING LIAISON GROUP
   Robert C. Birney (Chairman, LRPC Group II)
   North Burn (Chairman, LRPC)
   Kathie R. Florsheim (Chairman, Five College Student Coordinating Board—Mount Holyoke, '69)
   Prosser Gifford (Chairman, LRPC Group I)
   Charles Henderson, Jr. (Chairman, LRPC Group III)
   Joseph B. Kilmartin, Jr. (FCSCB Member—University, '69)
   Diane E. Martin (FCSCB Secretary—Mount Holyoke, '70)
   Pamela Myers (FCSCB Treasurer, later Chairman—Smith, '70)
   Joshua L. Posner (FCSCB Member—Amherst, '69)
   Mark C. Smith (FCSCB Member—University, '71)

2. FINE ARTS
   Amherst—Frank A. Trapp (Professor of Fine Arts), Scott O. Wilson, '69
   Hampshire—Francis D. Smith (Dean of School of Humanities and Arts)
   Mount Holyoke—Jean C. Harris (Associate Professor of Art), Phyllis A. Bogard, '69
   Smith—Richard J. Judson (Professor of Art), Judith L. Thieme, '71
   University—Paul E. Norton (Professor of Art), Bonita Cohn, '69

3. Performing Arts
   Amherst—Walter L. Boughton (Professor of Dramatic Arts), Craig F. Dunkerley, '69
   Hampshire—Francis D. Smith (Dean of School of Humanities and Arts)
   Mount Holyoke—Ronald Hodges (Associate Professor of Music), Elizabeth E. Graff, '70
   Smith—Helen K. Chinoy (Associate Professor of Theatre and Speech), Karen S. Crow, '71
   University—Harry P. Mahnken (Assistant Professor of Speech), Elaine S. Rickless, '71

4. Film
   Amherst—James H. Bierman (Assistant Professor of Dramatic Arts), E. Reeves Callaway, '70
   Hampshire—Francis D. Smith (Dean of School of Humanities and Arts)
   Mount Holyoke—James D. Ellis (Associate Professor of English), Katherine M. Mezur, '71, Ronnie Greenfield, '71
   Smith—George Cohen (Professor of Art), Carol Reis, '72
   University—Richard L. Stromgren (Instructor of Speech), Harriet Lipnik, '71

5. Student Life
   Amherst—Robert A. Ward (Dean of Students), Scott F. Turow, '70, P. Scott McGee, '70
   Hampshire—David Matz (Assistant to the President)
   Mount Holyoke—Ruth E. Warfel (Dean of Students), Judith Harris, '70, Julie A. Wortman, '70
   Smith—Helen L. Russell (Dean of Students), S. Hart Brent, '71, Paula Hendricks, '69
   University—William F. Field (Dean of Students), Joseph B. Kilmartin, Jr., '69, Paul J. Silverman, '69

6. Student Exchange
   Amherst—Robert F. Grose (Registrar), Frederick E. Hoxie, '69, David T. Moore, '69
   Hampshire—Richard C. Lyon (Dean of the College)
   Mount Holyoke—Anne C. Edmonds (Librarian), Clara

R. Ludwig (Director of Admissions), Kathie R. Florsheim, '69

Smith—Patricia C. Olmsted (Assistant Dean), Paula Hendricks, '69, Ida E. Offenbach, '69

University—William C. Venman (Assistant Dean of Administration), Joseph B. Kilmartin, Jr., '69

7. MENTAL HEALTH SERVICES

Amherst—Haskell R. Coplin (Professor of Psychology and Student Counselor)

Hampshire—Robert C. Birney (Dean of School of Social Science)

Mount Holyoke—Carol E. Craig (Director of Health Service and College Physician)

Smith—Vera Joseph (Director of Health Service and College Physician)

University—Harold Jarmon (Associate Professor of Psychology), Julian F. Janowitz (Director of Mental Health Services)

D. Committees recommended by the LRPC and established by the Presidents

1. REGIONAL & ENVIRONMENTAL PLANNING COMMITTEE

Amherst—Kurt M. Hertzfeld (Treasurer)

Hampshire—Charles R. Longsworth (Vice President)

Mount Holyoke—Lawrence E. Remillard (Comptroller)

Smith—Jack W. Simpkin (Associate Treasurer)

University—Ervin H. Zube (Professor of Landscape Architecture)

2. FIELD OFFICE FOR URBAN & REGIONAL STUDIES

Amherst—Hadley Arkes (Assistant Professor of Political Science)

Hampshire—Robert C. Birney (Dean of School of Social Science)

Mount Holyoke—Sarah S. Montgomery (Associate Professor of Economics and Sociology)

Smith—Ely Chinoy (Professor of Sociology and Anthropology)
University—Philip B. Coulter (Assistant Professor of Government)

Acknowledgements

It would be impossible to mention all the people who have given the Long Range Planning Committee the benefit of their time and thought. The members of the formal committees established by or on the recommendation of the LRPC (listed in the preceding section) spent many hours in meetings. The sections of this report dealing with the subjects they discussed are based to a great extent on their recommendations. Members of other five-college standing committees and groups—the Five College Student Coordinating Board, the Five College Committee on Social Responsibility, the Librarians, who not only met together to prepare recommendations but also met with the LRPC as a whole for a long session, the Registrars, the Directors of Admissions, the Development Officers, the Secretaries of the institutions and, of course, the Deputies—also contributed significantly. Barbara B. Burn, Director of International Programs at the University, Philip B. Coulter, Assistant Professor of Government at the University, and Ruth C. Lawson, Professor of Political Science at Mount Holyoke, prepared individual draft papers for the consideration of the LRPC. Robert F. Grose, Registrar and Associate Professor of Psychology at Amherst, and Robert G. Cope, Director of Institutional Studies at the University, prepared a proposal for obtaining an inventory of faculty resources. Murray J. Kiteley, Professor of Philosophy at Smith, read an early draft of the report and made a number of useful suggestions.

The Committee had the benefit of excellent facilities for its work. Hampshire College provided a conference room for biweekly meetings. The Northfield Inn was most accommodating for three several-day sessions and The Highpoint Inn in Lenox for one session.

The highly competent staff is listed above, and the special help of Barbara Turlington is mentioned as well in the Letter of Transmittal. Mrs. Nora Fornas, in addition to her secretarial duties, also provided most of the dinners at our evening meetings. Mrs. Edith Heath was a most helpful and flexible part-time typist. Mrs. Toni Beckwith, our copy editor, greatly improved the report while working under the pressure of stringent deadlines and the problems caused by multiple authorship.

We very much appreciate the help given by Mrs. Leone Stein, Director of the University of Massachusetts Press, and other members of the staff in the publication and distribution of the report. Special thanks are due to Richard Hendel for designing the report.

A grant of $5,000 from the United States Steel Foundation in 1968 helped significantly with the costs of preparing this report, and a grant of $100,000 in 1969 from the Richard King Mellon Charitable Trusts will be used to help carry out some of the recommendations concerning academic cooperation and future planning. To both foundations the LRPC gives special thanks.

Wherever the LRPC sought help, it was generously given. Students, faculty members, and administrative officers in all five colleges cooperated on this report, and the LRPC is convinced that this augurs well for its sympathetic reception and careful consideration.

All these people, and more, helped, but the members of the Long Range Planning Committee take sole responsibility for this report and for any errors of omission and commission it may contain.